Thriving as a Mom without a Mom

Guidance for moms who don't have a supportive mother by their side

Melissa E. D. Reilly, Psy.D.

ISBN 979-8-9880243-0-9 Paperback
ISBN 979-8-9880243-1-6 Ebook

PRAISE FOR

THRIVING AS A MOM WITHOUT A MOM

"This book is a game-changer for anyone navigating the complex journey of motherhood without their own mom by their side. Dr. Reilly's "three parts of thriving" framework provides practical tools and strategies for understanding grief, building a support system, and finding joy in motherhood. With her heartfelt writing and compassionate perspective, this book is an invaluable resource for mothers and those supporting them through this deeply personal journey."
—Adrianne Hart, CHt, adriannehart.com

Thriving as a Mom Without a Mom should be read by every single woman, especially those with moms. I was drawn in by Melissa's powerful stories. I couldn't put the book down, almost like it was a novel and I wanted to see how it unfolded. She masterfully mixes vivid storytelling with practical application. What a wonderful book that will forever make me appreciate that I had a mom during my early mom years." **—Dana Malstaff, founder Boss Mom LLC**

"Melissa's insights have been powerful for me in understanding my own story of raising my baby oceans away from my own mother. She shares essential wisdom on recognizing grief and building helpful relationships. If only I'd had her book as a new mother!" **—Fiona Valentine, Business School for Artists and author of *Tiny Wings***

"This book validates the unique challenges we (as moms without moms) don't always even know how to articulate and lovingly guides us along the journey to healing. I appreciated hearing her personal journey as well as gaining a deeper understanding of some of the loneliness I went through on my own journey as a mom without a mom for the past 22 years. If you've lost your mom in any way, and you're on your own journey of motherhood, you will want to get this book." **—Nicole Terrell, Sensuality Coach**

"*Thriving As A Mom Without A Mom* is a must-read for any mom who is raising her children without her own mother by her side. Motherhood without the guidance and support of a loving, seasoned mom to lean on is undoubtedly a unique experience that only moms without moms can understand. Mothering while grieving comes with challenges that many of our fellow mom peers just can't relate to. Melissa beautifully weaves her own personal experiences with loss, grief, and the experience of motherhood without her mom with practical guidance for readers to better navigate their unique challenges. I have never read anything more validating and more helpful in regards to being a mom without a mom. Whether you're estranged from your mom, she's not able to be physically present for you, or she's passed on, *Thriving As A Mom Without A Mom* provides the support and guidance you've likely been craving." —**Emilie Delworth, Author, Trauma Recovery and Parenting Coach**

"Melissa so graciously captures the experience of being a mom without a mom. She expertly takes us on a journey through her own experiences and provides us with the information needed to get through the grief process. She shows us that even though our moms aren't with us to help us with being a mom, we can build a community to fill that "relationship gap". Melissa does a wonderful job showing new moms and all moms who have lost their own moms, how to build a mom identity that brings joy to being a mom. I will highly recommend this book in both my therapy practice and coaching practice." —**Denise Takakjy MC, LPC, NCC, CATP, BSL, Licensed professional counselor, Certified parent coach, Healing Hearts Healthy Minds Counseling Services PLLC, Parenting the Peaceful Way Parent Coaching**

"If you're like me as a mom without a mom and find yourself feeling a bit afraid, isolated, and longing for your mom to help you ease the pain, you'll find comfort and strength in this book. Melissa strikes the perfect balance between sharing what she's learned from her own experience as a mom without a mom, providing helpful insights from other motherless moms, and offering practical strategies that can truly change your life. Having known Melissa for her whole life, I continue to be amazed by her strength and fortitude, her ability to make the best out of difficult situations, and her heartfelt desire to help others by sharing what she's learned from her own story. Melissa is an inspiration to me, and I have no doubt her book will be an inspiration to you on your own mom journey." —**Her loving Aunt Sandra**

TABLE OF CONTENTS

DEDICATION

I dedicate this book to Jackson and Tommy;
it is the two of you who inspire me to be
the best mom I can be!

In memory of my mom, for whom I will
always be grateful!

CHAPTER 1

INTRODUCTION

As I write this, the holidays have recently passed, and I love being a mom and an entrepreneur. My son Jackson is active in his elementary school musical, frequently hangs out with a lovely group of friends, and has been having fun creating animations that he proudly displays at school. My psychological practice is thriving, and I am passionate about my new coaching program for moms without a mom.

But it wasn't always like this.

Unfortunately, the first few years of my son's life were among the most challenging times of mine. I felt utterly alone and completely lost about how to be a mom. My mother and two sisters had died before he was born, and I'd lived in our town for less than a year.

I had been a clinical psychologist for over 10 years and knew a lot about human development, parenting, and relationship dynamics. I assisted hundreds of moms as they worked through their insecurities about being new parents. But unfortunately, none of that prepared me for the utter inadequacy I felt when my son was born.

There were many times when I was suddenly and unexpectedly faced with something I didn't know anything about. I couldn't believe how difficult this was and how uncharacteristically clueless I felt as a mother.

I was a successful psychologist, a business owner, and a mature woman who was confident in who she was as a woman, yet I couldn't handle being a mom. During the first couple of years of my son's life, I was ashamed and often embarrassed by what I saw as my mothering incompetence. What in the world was wrong with me?

Jackson was born with neurological conditions that took a year to diagnose and required years of intensive therapies to engage in basic tasks, including walking, talking, and interacting with others in meaningful ways. I was filled with fear and self-blame (completely irrational) and felt utterly overwhelmed. Being a shy introvert made reaching out for help challenging. I felt like something was wrong with me because it felt like I was failing as a mom.

And then I realized that I felt different because I was different. There are unique challenges that all moms without a mom experience that impacts their mothering. I knew I needed help. I couldn't do it alone. So, here is what I did:

1. I replaced my negative self-talk with compassion and encouragement.

2. I educated myself about the challenges my son and I were facing and what we needed to do.

3. I sought emotional support from people who would listen rather than try to cheer me up or give advice.

4. I asked for assistance from people who could lighten the load.

I continued to treat clients after my son was born, and my practice included a large number of moms. It took a few years, but I started noticing several common factors among the other mothers I was treating who also didn't have a mom in their life.

So, I started thinking about how moms who don't have the support and guidance of a loving mom in their day-to-day life experience unique challenges that largely go unrecognized. As the psych nerd that I am, I did some research and didn't find much.

At that point, I realized I was developing a framework that identified those differences and would create a process to help those moms feel confident, secure, and supported in their mothering journey even though they didn't have their own mothers to lean on.

I want all moms to thrive and recognize their inner strength, especially moms like me who don't have a loving and supportive mom in their day-to-day lives, which is why I am writing this book.

In *Thriving As A Mom Without A Mom*, I share my story in detail and share the experiences of women who graciously opened up to me for the purpose of this book. All names in this book have been changed to maintain their privacy. Furthermore, I lay out the framework I have created to help all moms without a mom go from feeling isolated, overwhelmed, and insecure to feeling confident, supported, and secure as they thrive.

CHAPTER 2

WILL A BABY BE BORN

The Unexpected Surprise

The moment I became pregnant for the first time, I was shocked, terrified, and embarrassed. I was in the process of ending a relationship that wasn't working, and I was utterly unprepared to become a mom. I was one month shy of my 36th birthday. How in the world did this happen? I simultaneously wanted to call my mom and was relieved that I didn't have to face her with this news. That fear of disappointing my mom was still intense, even though it was more than 10 years after her death.

I had so many questions for her. But most of all, I wanted her to tell me that everything would be okay. I wanted her to encourage me and support me. I needed her to build me up at that moment. But she wasn't there. I was alone.

I made the decision to go alone to my first OB appointment. I wanted this to be a memorable experience for my little one and me, and I had no desire to share that moment with my soon-to-be ex-boyfriend. Frankly, I didn't want any distractions from the remarkable process of being pregnant with my first child.

The nurse began the vaginal ultrasound, and I eagerly awaited to see the little bean-sized baby. Moments dragged out into minutes. Her face went from pleasant and smiling to severe and quiet. What did this mean? She excused herself, and in came my OB. I wasn't expecting him to be part of the ultrasound. He then continued with the ultrasound procedure.

After an eternity, he said, "I am sorry, but your pregnancy is not progressing."

I didn't know what that meant. What? How could this be?

Sadly, I lost that baby at 10 weeks. I had support and kindness from my father, stepmother, Aunt Sandra, and friends. But, truth be told, I longed to be held and rocked by my mom. I wanted her soft, comforting shoulder to cry on. But it wasn't there. So, of course, I muddled through.

I was happy with my career and felt confident as a woman. My life felt whole, and becoming a mother didn't seem like it was in the cards for me. However, the loss of my first pregnancy highlighted how much I wanted a baby and how much I had been suppressing this desire to manage the sad thought that I would never have a family of my own.

Shortly after the miscarriage, I ended the relationship and quickly began another. But this time, I was actively seeking a relationship for the purpose of marriage and having children. I'd believed for most of my adult life that I wasn't supposed to have children. My ex-husband, from whom I had been divorced for several years, made it clear that, in his opinion, given the medical and mental health history of my family, I should not have children. I could see his point and never challenged that belief. However, my first pregnancy and subsequent loss made me realize how important having a child was to me.

I became pregnant again pretty quickly. I was shocked. Like many women who go years without becoming pregnant, I assumed I was sterile. I was wrong.

Although not planned or expected, the second pregnancy was a joyous occasion. Tom and I were in love and quickly became engaged. I wished I could tell my mother the news with excitement this time. But instead, I began fantasizing about all the conversations we would have had about my pregnancy. Unfortunately, a month after finding out I was pregnant, I miscarried again. The grief was intense, but we distracted ourselves with wedding plans.

I became pregnant the second month after our wedding. So much for the statistics indicating that fertility starts declining in our mid-thirties. I was anxiously excited this time. We were married, I felt prepared to be a mom, and knew this was what I wanted. And yet again, I miscarried.

Now, I was devastated. Why was this happening? Three years prior, I was comfortable with the notion that I would never have children. And now, I knew how badly I wanted to be a mom and how devastating it was to keep having these losses. I longed to talk with my mom about her miscarriage and the death of my older sister Kim who died when we were young children (more about this later). I wanted to have that partner in grief that is unique among moms.

At the follow-up appointment following the miscarriage, my OB scheduled us for anatomical testing to help identify potential causes for the multiple miscarriages. She informed us that the first test was a uterine scan to rule out the presence of a uterine malformation that could be causing the miscarriages. We were told that this test couldn't be performed on a pregnant woman, so she recommended we protect against pregnancy. A negative pregnancy test was obtained at that appointment, and the uterine scan was scheduled for two weeks later. The following week,

I felt pregnancy symptoms. Sure enough, I was pregnant again — despite our attempts to avoid pregnancy.

Labor Begins Too Soon

Needless to say, I was filled with dread. I couldn't bear the thought of losing another pregnancy. Again, I wanted my mom more than ever. Each week went by, and I continued to be pregnant. Finally, at our six-week appointment, we heard a heartbeat. We cried. At eight weeks, there was still a heartbeat. At 10 weeks, the ultrasound looked normal. I couldn't believe it; this might be okay.

We passed the first trimester without incident and entered the second trimester. I was still an anxious mess. I had a procedure on my cervix in my early thirties that mildly increased my risk of cervical insufficiency, also known as an incompetent cervix. This is when the cervix opens prematurely, often leading to a second-trimester loss.

Given that I was 37 years old, had three prior miscarriages, had a hypothyroid disorder, and had a previous cervical procedure, I was being monitored closely by fetal-maternal medicine. This is a group of physicians who specialize in high-risk pregnancies and medical complications during pregnancy.

In August, I was at my routine 26-week appointment with fetal-maternal medicine, getting another 3D ultrasound. Both my husband Tom and my four-year-old stepson Tommy came along, and we were excited to see the baby and get more pictures of our little one. However, during the ultrasound, the nurse noticed something and excused herself. My heart started to race. This had yet to happen at any of our previous appointments.

A few moments later, the physician came in and performed the ultrasound. He took many pictures and measurements. My heart began to sink, and my eyes filled with tears. I looked over at my husband and saw the glistening in his eyes. My hyperactive stepson was stone still. He sensed something was wrong. What had started as a fun and exciting appointment became a nightmare for the three of us.

After an eternity of silent poking, prodding, and clicking on the computer, the doctor informed me that my cervix was beginning to thin and dilate. He ordered a stress test immediately and sent me to the next room with Tom and Tommy in tow.

The nurse put several monitors on my abdomen and back while I remained on the table. After about 10 minutes, the doctor returned and told me that I was having contractions at regular intervals. I had no idea that the back pain I had been feeling for days was contractions.

At that moment, it felt like the world had stopped. I could hear the rushing of blood in my ears and the panic rising in my chest. I felt like I couldn't breathe. Then I felt my husband's hand firmly grip my arm. He leaned down, kissed my cheek, and said it would be okay. It was a lifeline keeping me from being pulled into a whirlpool in the middle of an abyss.

I was in pre-term labor. The office was located within the Women and Babies Hospital, so they took me down on a gurney to the emergency room and started the admissions process. My time in the ER was a blur. I have very little memory of that time, as I was in shock. I changed into a hospital gown, and my husband called his ex-wife so she could take my stepson home with her.

IVs were inserted, and countless nurses and aides were getting me situated and asking what felt like a million questions. I was in a daze. At one point, they informed me that they needed to administer a series of steroid shots to boost the baby's lungs in case I delivered that night. My OB entered the room and told me what the plan was. I would remain in the hospital while receiving a series of shots that included steroids and several other medications to stop the labor. She told me the treatment would feel awful, but we needed to stop the labor because the survival rate at 26 weeks was only 50%.

How was this happening? I was still in the second trimester, for goodness' sake.

What did I do to deserve so much loss in my life?

Once again, I felt like my life was falling apart and I didn't have my mom. I prayed my little heart out. And every few hours, I gave thanks that I was still pregnant and the baby was still alive and growing.

The hours crept by, and another shot was administered. Hours turned into days, and my pregnancy continued. As the shock and terror of it all began to diminish, all of the other factors I needed to deal with came crashing down. At this moment, I began to feel the full impact of becoming a mom without my own mom's assistance.

I am a psychologist and a co-owner of a group practice. I had a full-time caseload at the time. My clients needed to be told (some of them didn't even know I was pregnant) that I would be out for a while, since telemedicine wasn't a thing yet. Thankfully, my business partner was one of my close friends and graciously handled most of the things related to the practice that needed to be addressed.

This all felt overwhelming, to say the least.

Shame Becomes My New Companion

After a week in the hospital, I was allowed to go home on strict bed rest. I was not prepared for this. We had three dogs, my stepson Tommy lived with us 50% of the time, and my husband Tom was returning to work soon.

How was I going to manage? This was one of the loneliest times of my life.

Neither my husband nor I had family in the state and, as I mentioned earlier, I was new to the town. There wasn't anyone I felt I could turn to for help. I had never needed my mother's emotional support, assistance, and guidance as much as I did at that moment.

I was alone all day with fear, discomfort, and a general negative feeling that I didn't recognize at the time as shame. I felt helpless. Every move I made felt like I was endangering the life of my unborn child.

But I was alone. I had to get out of bed to go to the bathroom, get food, and let the dogs out. My husband could only do so much to help me get situated before he left for work. I felt like I was endangering the baby no matter what I did.

I constantly judged every little thing I did. The mom's guilt was intense, and I had never even held my baby. The fact that I had no one to talk to about this made it even worse.

Most people saw me as competent, strong, and well-adjusted. No one knew that I was suffering inside. I thought that something must be wrong with me.

Why was this happening? I must have caused all of this bad stuff to be happening. Despite the irrational nature of these thoughts, I couldn't help but feel them.

So, I began to talk with my mom. I just started telling her everything. I had a running conversation with her in my head and, sometimes, on paper. I found some comfort in this.

I was still angry with her (I will explain more about this later), but I could slowly feel comforted by her as well. My mom had been dead for over 10 years. But I needed her now more than ever.

I thanked God for every day that I remained pregnant. Each

day I was pregnant meant another day that my little baby boy was developing.

I was seen twice weekly, once by my regular OB and once by fetal-maternal medicine. Every appointment involved myriad measurements and scans. I wasn't surprised when the nurse informed me that I still had contractions; I could feel them, and they became my constant companion. They never stopped.

I was told that given the measurements of my cervix and other factors, the chance of carrying my son to term was only 10%. Some visits to fetal-maternal medicine were reassuring; others resulted in another visit to the emergency room, more shots, and an intense fear that things were falling apart.

As each appointment or passing of another pregnancy milestone, I was relieved that my son was growing and developing. However, I was becoming terrified about the birth. Because I was on bedrest, I could not attend birth classes, get a tour of the delivery room, or take part in any of the other pre-birth rituals that first-time mamas go through. This was before virtual classes or courses were a thing, so I didn't have access to any virtual options.

Again, I was completely alone. I didn't have my mom, grandmothers, or sisters to ask questions or get the intimate details of what to expect. I was on my own, I knew it, and I felt lost.

To mitigate my growing fear, I read as many books about pregnancy, birth, and taking care of babies as possible. Of course, the nerd in me was helped by all of my reading, but my emotional side wasn't. The books couldn't hug me, hold my hand, or wipe my tears away.

In many ways, I felt forgotten. For example, there needed to be someone to give me a baby shower. My supportive business partner intended to have one for me, but it was canceled once I was on bed rest. Looking back, it seems like such a trivial thing, but at the time, I felt so sad that I was missing out on yet another female rite of passage.

But I kept praying and was determined to muster the best attitude. I was thankful for the friends I had, my husband, and our extended family. I looked forward to being a mom and was becoming increasingly excited despite my fear.

My Bedrest Is Done, And I'm Back To Work For A Week

I made it to week 36. I couldn't believe it. My OB congratulated us at that appointment and informed me that I was officially off bed rest. In fact, she wanted me to start moving my body gently to build up some strength for delivery. When you are on bed rest, the muscles in your body wither and shrink because they aren't being used. I was weak and generally uncomfortable all over. But I was excited. And now, officially nine months pregnant.

Tom and I began going on short little walks with the dogs. Then, I went to our rec center and went for a swim. That was the weirdest sensation, being in the water and feeling the contractions. But I kept moving. Each day, it felt like I was getting more robust and less winded.

I was told I could go to work for a few hours a day if I chose. So, I scheduled a week to see the clients who needed to be seen. Unfortunately, my office is an hour from home, so the drive was nerve-racking.

In one week, I had two trips to the hospital as my labor pains had increased. So, we made the decision for me to stop working again. But at least I was able to get a little done before delivering.

Halloween arrived, and my stepson Tommy was excited to dress in his skeleton costume and go trick-or-treating. I was thrilled because I was allowed to walk around with him. It was a fun evening. But at the end of it, I started getting more muscular contractions and thought again that the baby was coming.

We were experts when it came to hopping in the car and going to the Women and Babies Hospital. But this was the first time we went knowing they wouldn't do anything to stop the labor. We were excited.

We went and, several hours later, we were sent home. On our way home, we passed through a DUI checkpoint; it was 1 am on Halloween, after all. The officers asked where we were coming from. When my husband responded, two flashlights went right to my belly. It was pretty comical. They let us pass without any other questions.

The next several days were painful and scary. I was four centimeters dilated, fully effaced, and the baby was engaged. The baby was in position and ready to arrive, yet labor was not progressing. I was sent home after several hours each time I went in, which was every day at that point. Each day the contractions would strengthen, and the time between them shortened. It was getting close, and I finally felt ready.

From 5 Centimeters To 9 Centimeters In 20 Minutes

One Wednesday morning early in November, I awoke at 5 am from a painful set of contractions. These were the strongest I had felt so far. Tom had a meeting he needed to attend, but made arrangements with his school that he would come home after the meeting and take me to the hospital.

On the way to the hospital, with tears in my eyes, I told him, "I can't come home today. This has to be it."

I was scared.

We got there, and I was discouraged to hear I was still at four centimeters. I couldn't believe it.

My OB sent me to the delivery intake unit and instructed me to walk and use the yoga ball. After an hour of this, she congratulated me and said I was at five centimeters and would not leave the hospital until I delivered.

It was mid-afternoon when I called my father, who was living in Poughkeepsie, New York at the time. He and his wife would leave and meet us in the hospital in the morning. I so wished that my mother was there with me.

I was ecstatic. My doctor gave me an estimated one to two hours per centimeter for typical labor. I was still in the intake area, and the orders were written for me to be admitted into labor and delivery.

Ironically, my water broke in a forceful gush within minutes of the doctor leaving the room. It literally felt like something broke when the flood came during a contraction.

The staff was preparing to move me, and I stated that I would walk. I had gone less than 10 steps and felt pain like I had never felt. Thank goodness Tom was there to hold me up. It was the kind of pain that was blinding and disorienting. I literally couldn't move.

They got the gurney, and I asked for an epidural as they rolled me into the room where I would go into labor and then deliver my son. I thought there was no way I could withstand that kind of pain for 10 hours.

The nurse began asking the standard intake questions as I entered the room. But I couldn't speak. She looked at me and told me to stop pushing. I hadn't realized I was.

She did an internal exam and stated, "Well, that was fast; you are at 9 ½ centimeters."

The baby was on its way. I was at 4 centimeters for a week, went to 5 centimeters in an hour, my water broke, and in 20 minutes, I went from 5 to 9 ½ centimeters.

I felt a mix of panic and excitement. I was terrified that something was going wrong. I was paranoid that I would do a bad thing.

When I could talk, I whispered, "I don't know what to do."

The nurse said, "Breathe and push when you feel like it."

Tom had to answer all of the intake questions because, at this point, I had gone inward. The epidural was canceled because it was too late. This was going to be a natural birth.

As the contractions intensified and I was in the throes of labor, I feared my pelvis fracturing. Okay, I know that seems dramatic — but when I was 16 years old, I was in a traumatic vehicle accident that resulted in three pelvis fractures, among other injuries. One of my clearest memories of that incident was going to a six-month follow-up with the orthopedist and overhearing the doctor quietly telling my mom that childbirth shouldn't be an issue. I never forgot that and, in the back of my mind, I continued to fear it.

The doctor entered the room, gowned up, and got into position. I delivered my precious little boy at 5:01 pm, within a few minutes of the doctor's arrival. I was in awe. I couldn't believe it had finally happened, and everything was ok. I carried Jackson to 37 weeks; he was born healthy at a little over six pounds.

My Son, Me, And Grief Spend The Night Together

Shortly after I delivered, I signed the intake paperwork, and they rolled my son and me to our room. Besides being sore in all the expected areas, I felt great! I was alert, attentive, and, above all, relieved. My son was alive, well, and here with me. At that moment, all felt right with the world.

After about an hour, Tom left to Pick-up Tommy to meet his newborn brother Jackson. I was alone with Jackson. And then a new kind of fear crept in. At that moment, I realized I had never even held a newborn before. Everything was completely new to me. My education and background in teaching human development didn't matter at that moment. I felt completely lost.

We have all heard stories of people counting their baby's fingers and toes. Not me. I was too overwhelmed. I felt frozen with fear that I would do something wrong. I recognize now just how out of proportion that fear was.

I then began to notice a vast flood of longing for my mom. My thoughts went to her often in those first few hours. It felt like I didn't have anyone to turn to and, literally, in those first few hours, I didn't. Of course, I had the nurses and doctors all there and happy to assist; they answered my questions as they popped up. But the truth was, I was too embarrassed by what I saw as my absolute incompetence to relax enough to ask all of my questions.

After about an hour and a half, Tom and Tommy came in and happy introductions took place. Tom had been through this and was comfortable and confident in his role as a father. I hid the intensity of my fear from him because it didn't seem as if he would understand.

Unfortunately, this began an unhealthy pattern of keeping my fears to myself, and there they festered into feelings of shame. It felt like a terrible secret that no one would understand. My motherhood journey had just begun, and already I felt overwhelmed, insecure, alone, and filled with shame and doubt.

CHAPTER 3

WHAT DOES IT MEAN TO BE A MOM WITHOUT A MOM

When I became pregnant for the first time, I joined an exclusive club. I didn't know this club existed, a club no one wants to be part of. What club is that, you ask? It is The Moms Without A Mom Club.

Who Has Access To The Moms Without A Mom Club?

Although it may seem obvious, there are several ways that you become a member of this exclusive club that nobody wants to join. Regardless of how you become a member, being part of this club makes you different from other moms. You don't look different, and oftentimes you don't even recognize the difference. But you feel it.

I define a mom without a mom as any mom who doesn't have the support and guidance of a loving mother by her side. Three primary ways this occurs are when a woman is separated from her mother by death, a dysfunctional or toxic relationship, or physical distance. At first glance, they appear to be vastly different circumstances. And in many ways, they are. But there are also significant similarities among members of these groups, which has led me to see them as sisters in this particular club.

Separated By Death

One way a mom can become a member of The Moms Without A Mom club is if she is separated from her mother by death. This includes women who lost their mothers when they were children or lost them later after becoming an adult. It doesn't matter if your mom met your children or if she died before their birth. Regardless, if your mom has passed, you are a mom without a mom.

The loss of a mother creates a significant impact on both adults and children. In fact, Umberson (2006) found that adults who lose their mother experience heightened levels of psychological distress (33), including marital deterioration (105) as well as increased use of food as a coping mechanism (41). In addition, parental distress and dysfunction negatively impact children within the household.

Early Life Loss Of Mom

Few things are more devastating to a child than losing their mother. In fact, the risk of mortality increases when a child's mother dies (Nguyen et al., 2019). Furthermore, the loss of a mother is associated with an increased risk for substance abuse and mental health disorders. In addition, later achievements in life, such as school performance and job placement, can be negatively impacted by the death of a mother during childhood (Ellis, Dowrick & Lloyd-Williams, 2013).

The love and support a mother provides her children are critical for building a sense of trust in the world, which becomes a foundational component in forming healthy adult relationships. We aren't born knowing how to be a mother. We learn from our own experiences of being mothered and from other mothers, primarily our own.

So, what happens when you don't have a mother as a child? You learn from what you observe from others, which in large part depends on the people who filled any mothering role in your life. Children with other family members who are warm, caring, compassionate, and consistent do better than those who don't (Ellis, Dowrick & Lloyd-Williams, 2013).

Loss Of Mom In Adulthood

I was 25 years old when my mother passed away. I was an adult on my way to start the life I had been working so hard at creating. I was in a long-term committed relationship, nearly finished with my doctoral degree, and was in the process of securing my first position as a psychologist. My life was starting just as my mother's life abruptly ended.

Regardless of your age when your mom dies, there are many life experiences that you wish your mom could be a part of. Weddings, births, graduations, and myriad firsts, each containing an aspect of grief because your mother isn't celebrating with you.

If your mom dies before your first child, there is always a sense of something missing during your pregnancy and birth experience.

Hailey had her first child five years after her mother passed away.

She recalled, "I first started crying in labor and never stopped. I had intense grief over not having my mom to share this with. I felt terrible guilt. I couldn't make milk. I had postpartum depression and needed to be hospitalized when the baby was five weeks old."

Hailey's experience is not unusual. The newborn stage is particularly triggering for those whose mother has died.

If your mother dies after you've had children, her death marks a significant milestone in your and your children's lives. The time when Grandma was alive and the time after she died. There is sorrow for what she will miss and what the kids will miss in not having her around. There is the added difficulty of needing to assist them with the grief process while you are grieving yourself.

Separated By Emotional Estrangement Or Abandonment

This is a large and diverse group of women. Unfortunately, not all of us have had great experiences with our mothers. You may be one of the many women who have experienced intergenerational cycles of abuse or trauma. Toxic relationships can be passed down through the generations until awareness builds and the complicated process of breaking these cycles begins.

Sadly, there's a significant number of children who've been abandoned by their mothers. In 2020 alone, approximately 250,000 children were victims of abuse or neglect at the hands of their mothers. (U.S. Department of Health and Human Services, 2022). In addition, the relationship someone has with their mother in childhood significantly impacts later life relationships, including with their children.

Abusive relationships with someone's mother can also occur in adulthood. This often is quite painful for the daughter and impacts her later attachments with children.

Emotional estrangement occurs when a woman has had to make the tough decision to end a toxic or abusive relationship. Even when you are the one ending a relationship and making this difficult choice, having to do so is still painful. After all, we are hardwired to desire a connection with our mothers. No one wants to be estranged from her mother. You choose it because staying in the relationship is even more painful.

The severance of the mother-daughter relationship, even when the relationship is toxic, goes against our biology. Unfortunately, when the relationship is abusive, the healthiest choice is to disconnect.

Olivia, whose mother was in and out of her life from the beginning, stated, "The toxic nature of her relationship has had more of an impact than the actual absence of her."

Olivia made the difficult decision to go no contact for the past 18 months and despite missing her mother, she knows her decision was what was best for her and her family.

Not having her mom in her life, despite the fact that she is alive, left another woman, Darla, feeling isolated.

She said, "It's been hard. When I first became a mom, it took a very long time to finally accept that I don't have a mom to go to. I would feel so insecure as a mother because I didn't have a mom to back me up."

Separation By Physical Distance

Shortly after I was born, my parents moved to a rural area in upstate New York, three hours away from their parents. Finally, they could purchase property, build a house, and raise their children in an environment they believed would be better than where they grew up.

From the time I was young, I remember my parents talking about when we grew up and moved away. I thought all children grew up and moved away from their parents. Then, in my senior year of college, I discovered that most people stay where they grew up. This seemed so weird to me.

About 45% of American families live over an hour away from extended family, even though about 80% of women report that it's important to them to live near family (Hurst, 2022). Furthermore, the percentage of women moving away increases as the level of educational attainment rises. In other words, a woman with an advanced degree is more likely to live farther away from home than a woman with a high school diploma.

There are several special populations of moms in which separation from their families is typical. All three of these families face the unique challenge of raising their children in potentially different cultures.

The first group includes women who are part of the armed services and those whose life partner is in the military. This group of women face the added challenge of multiple moves and the inherent uncertainties that all military families encounter (Stilwell, 2023).

Another group commonly away from their family is members of international school systems. These are American educators who move to foreign countries to teach other American nationals who are living abroad.

The third common circumstance includes families who embark on missionary work. The time away from their family of origin can range from a brief period to many years.

What Do Moms Separated From Their Mom By Death, Distance, And Emotional Estrangement Have In Common?

At first glance, women's experiences among these three groups are significantly different. And while there are challenges unique to each group that I will discuss shortly, there are three factors that all three of the above categories of moms have in common.

1. Moms without a mom experience a grief process related to not having the support and guidance of a loving mom in their day-to-day life.

2. Moms without a mom don't have an easily identifiable "go-to" person that moms typically function as.

3. Moms without a mom experience a disruption in creating a mom identity.

These common factors are significant enough for me to view the group as a whole rather than as distinct. I will discuss each of these factors in depth in subsequent chapters. Now, I will turn to some of the crucial differences among the groups.

What Are The Particular/Unique Challenges For Each Group?

Separated By Death

There is an expected grief process you go through when you experience the death of a loved one. So, of course, it's no surprise that one would have a significant grief experience upon the passing of their mother. However, the grief process is a very individualized experience. Therefore, I will spend the next chapter discussing grief as it relates to losing one's mother.

Separation by death is the group most people think about when they hear the term, moms without a mom. Death is eternal, marks a final goodbye, and there is no hope of reconnection during this lifetime.

Separated By Emotional Estrangement Or A Toxic Relationship

Unfortunately, not all mother/daughter relationships are healthy. Some children have the unfortunate experience of being raised by an emotionally unhealthy mom. For some, the impact is mild and there can be a meaningful, even if not wholly fulfilling or enjoyable, relationship as the daughter becomes an adult. However, in severe circumstances, a complete severing of ties is initiated and maintained by either party.

Sadly, the grief process for women that fall into this category often goes unrecognized and leaves the women feeling unseen. Most adult women (80%-90%) have a secure emotional bond with their mothers (Fingerman, 2001). So, when you are one of the unfortunate ones who don't, you can feel isolated and alone.

The decision to separate yourself from your mother never comes easy. Even when you choose to leave a toxic relationship, you still grieve the loss of what you hoped you could have. Likewise, there is sorrow over what you thought might have been able to occur.

Carmen described a problematic relationship with her mother and said that they didn't have an emotional bond.

When asked if she recognized a grieving process, she stated, "No, I didn't recognize it as grief. I just got really sad about it. In my 40s, I felt disappointed. I've tried on my own to push through it. There are always milestones, reunions, and anniversaries that you want it to work out as 'normal,' but you don't have that."

How we see ourselves as a mom, parenting styles, and parenting values are all impacted by our own experiences of being mothered. When you are estranged from your mother, there is the added complication of wanting to provide a different experience for your children than what you had growing up. As a result, there can be a real struggle with identity. I will discuss the impacts of an emotionally unhealthy mom on the development of our mom identity in a later chapter of this book.

Several of the women I interviewed talked about how the harmful relationship they had with their mothers impacted their parenting as well as how they view themselves as a mother.

Darla stated, "It has impacted my relationship with my daughter in ways that haven't been there with my son."

Separated By Physical Distance

Although women in this group may be able to speak with their mothers, they still don't have easy access to their mothers daily. As a result, this group experiences frequent hellos and goodbyes that can be emotionally draining. There is also the added experience of worrying about being so far away from family if an emergency arises.

REFERENCES

Ellis, J., Dowrick, C. & Lloyd-Williams M. (2013, February) The long-term impact of early parental death: lessons from a narrative study. *Journal of the Royal Society of Medicine, 106, 2*. 57-67. https://pubmed.ncbi.nlm.nih.gov/23392851/

Fingerman, K. (2001). *Aging mothers and their adult daughters: A study of mixed emotions*. Springer Publishing Company.

Hurst, K. (2022). More than half of Americans live within an hour of extended family. *Pew Research Center*. Retrieved January 3, 2023 from https://www.pewresearch.org/fact-tank/2022/05/18/more-than-half-of-americans-live-within-an-hour-of-extended-family/

Nguyen, D. et al. (2019). Risk of childhood mortality associated with death of a mother in low-and-middle-income countries: a systematic review and meta-analysis. *BMC Public Health, 19, 1-21*.

Stilwell, B. (2023). 5 unique facts about military families and their children. *Pew Research Center*. Retrieved January 3, 2023 from https://www.pewresearch.org/fact-tank/2022/05/18/more-than-half-of-americans-live-within-an-hour-of-extended-family/

Umberson, D. (2006). *Death of a Parent: Transition To A New Adult Identity*. Cambridge University Press.

U.S. Department of Health and Human Services. (2022). Child Maltreatment 2020. Retrieved January 3, 2023 from https://www.acf.hhs.gov/cb/report/child-maltreatment-2020

CHAPTER 4

THE GRIEVING PROCESS

It was June 17, 1999, a Thursday, and my fiance and I were getting ready to go to my five-year college reunion at Elmira College. We were excited to meet up with my old college roommate Lorin and her husband Craig. It was going to be a fun time.

I received a call around 10 pm and heard my father's voice. I can't remember his exact words, but he told me my mother had just died.

I was confused. I didn't understand what he was saying. He told me she had a heart attack and died within moments. Apparently, it had just happened, and the authorities were not yet there.

My parents' house, my childhood home, was on top of a mountain in the Catskills Mountains of New York. It was a very rural area, and the nearest hospital or police organization was 40 minutes from our house. I imagined my mom sitting in her usual spot, appearing to be asleep, and I felt hollow inside.

From this moment forward, life was forever different. I no longer had my mom. The possibility of a close, loving relationship with her like I had when I was a child was gone forever. I felt lost. How was I going to navigate life without the support of my mom?

Within an hour of my return home, my dad and I left to tell my little sister Jennifer. She was living in an assisted living residence for individuals with psychological and intellectual challenges. My sister battled bipolar I disorder and was frequently hospitalized for psychiatric symptoms. She was thriving in her current housing situation, working part-time, having friends, and doing well in general. Both my father and I dreaded having to tell her.

We called the staff and alerted them to the situation. They would be present when we told my sister the news to provide any assistance if needed. I will never forget the pure joy on her face when she saw Dad and I arrive. She was so excited to see us and show me around (I had not seen her place yet as it was a relatively new placement, and I lived two states away). Seeing her so happy, knowing what I needed to tell her, broke my heart.

My father was silent. He couldn't speak.

I looked at my little sister's smiling face and calmly told her, "Jennifer, Mom died last night."

"No, she didn't. You're lying."

She stepped away from me in shock.

Again, I said, "I'm sorry, Jen, but I'm not lying. Mom had a heart attack last night and died."

At this point, Dad started crying and Jennifer screamed, "Nooooooo!"

That was one of the hardest things that I ever had to do.

The next several days were a blur of calling people with the news. Planning Mom's funeral. Making the many decisions that entails. Supporting my sister and father. The support from my college roommate Lorin and her husband Craig was crucial.

The night before the funeral, Lorin, Craig, my fiance, and I were sharing stories of my mom and reminiscing in general. The topic turned to the funeral the next day and who would give the eulogy. I asked several people to say something for the eulogy. Unfortunately, everyone responded that it would be too difficult for them to do.

Finally, Lorin kindly offered to say something for me. I will forever appreciate her willingness to step up in that way. But at that moment, I realized for the first time the depth and power of my inner strength. I knew I could and would give my mom's eulogy. It was a pivotal moment for me concerning self-confidence.

So, my sister Jennifer and I were tasked with speaking at my mother's funeral. I don't remember what either of us said, but I remember being immensely proud of my little sister. Despite her psychological illness, she also had inner strength passed down to us from our parents. My mother was the strongest person I knew, and now my sister and I were filling her shoes.

As most people learn after the death of a loved one, the challenging part starts after the funeral. The act of living without my mom was beginning. And I didn't know how to even start. So, I just muddled along the best I could.

Death Strikes Again

I was awakened by the telephone shortly before 5 am on Saturday morning, January 29, 2000. At the turn of the new millennium, everyone had landlines and cell phones were yet to be universal. I remember distinctly reaching over to the nightstand and feeling fear and sadness. I mean, no one calls in the middle of the night. In that brief millisecond before I said hello, I anticipated the news that my maternal grandmother had passed. She was in her upper 70s, and for most of her adult life, she had been "sickly."

With trepidation and in a sleep-fogged voice, I said, "Hello?"

A male stranger's voice asked, "Is this Melissa Derby (my maiden name)?"

What? I couldn't think.

By reflex, I answered him, "Yes, who is this?"

He introduced himself as my sister Jennifer's psychiatrist.

"I am so sorry, but your sister died a short time ago in her sleep."

It felt like time had stopped, and my thoughts came to a screeching halt. There was utter silence, both outside and inside my head. I couldn't process the words. It just didn't make sense.

After several seconds the man's voice asked if I was still on the line. That simple question acted like an on-switch, and everything started moving again. Nothing made sense, but I could think again.

My first question came out, "What happened?"

"She had a pulmonary embolism in her sleep."

"Where is she now?"

"She is here in the hospital."

He gave me some additional information, but I don't remember any of it. He then kindly asked If he could do anything for me.

"Yes, can you give me a number to reach you? I will call my father now; what number should I give him if he wants to talk with you?"

"Your father knows. I spoke with him already, and he asked me to call you."

"Oh...Thank you."

What a stupid thing for me to say. But that was what came out. After that, I ensured the psychiatrist knew that I was okay and I appreciated what he had just done for us. So here I was, I'd just heard the news that my sister is dead; it was just seven months after my mom died, and I was trying to take care of this stranger. I know it's crazy, but that was my default mode.

At this point, I heard my fiance muttering something. I couldn't tell what it was, but I believe he was trying to get confirmation of his belief that my grandmother had died. So, I tried to quiet him with a hand motion.

I heard the psychiatrist ask, "Can you come to the hospital? I will make myself available to you and your father today for any support you need. I have an outing with my family, but I will come in anytime you need."

"Yes, I will need to go get my dad and we will be there later today."

He gave me his contact information; I thanked him and got off the phone. Not a tear had yet been shed. I was in shock. I then had to relive the entire conversation with my fiance, who was stunned.

I then calmly called my father and told him I would be on my way in a few minutes. I was living in Pennsylvania, he was in upstate New York, and my sister had just died in Connecticut. At that moment, it felt like the three of us were a million miles apart.

My Identity As A Sister Was Gone

I had now lost my mother and both sisters, and my father was in despair. I was alone and lost. The experience of grief this time felt different. I hadn't realized how much my own identity was tied to being someone's sister. For the first time in my life, I wasn't anyone's sister. Jennifer and I were only 18 months apart. She was a massive part of my life, even though we were adults living in different states and leading very different lives. This just felt different.

I was now the sole female member of my nuclear family. However, it wasn't until years later, when I became pregnant, that the full impact of that fact became apparent. The pull for a female family connection is at its strongest when we are about to enter the uniquely female experience of being pregnant and giving birth. But, again, I was alone in this and, boy, did I feel it.

What Is Grief?

When we say grief, we typically think about mourning a death. However, grief occurs when we lose anything significant in our life. The American Psychological Association (APA) defines grief as:

> "the anguish experienced after significant loss, usually the death of a beloved person. Grief often includes physiological distress, separation anxiety, confusion, yearning, obsessive dwelling on the past, and apprehension about the future. Intense grief can become life-threatening through immune system disruption, self-neglect, and suicidal thoughts. Grief may also take the form of regret for something lost, remorse for something done, or sorrow for a mishap to oneself" (APA, 2022).

One of the hallmarks of grief is an intense feeling of yearning for what is lost. (O'Connor, 2022). There is a wish to have what we used to have or what we thought we would have. Unfortunately, this desire or yearning can become distracting and negatively impact our ability to experience our life as it presently is.

It is the loss of something significant that triggers grief. When a death occurs, we recognize our emotions as grief. However, if the loss isn't a death, like the loss of a desired relationship or the loss of physical connection, it is much harder to perceive our emotions as grief. Grief can also occur when we lose a future we hoped for; for example, having a mom in our life when we have children.

Stages Of Grief

The experience of grief is variable and changes with time. You may have heard that grief occurs in stages. This model was initially made famous by Elisabeth Kübler-Ross in 1969. The stages begin with a period of denial where the individual is in disbelief over what is occurring. The next stage is called anger, followed by bargaining, in which the individual tries to deal with their higher power to change the current situation. The next stage is depression, which includes periods of intense sadness. The final stage in this model is accepting the loss characterized by a decline in painful emotional experiences.

Unfortunately, when we think about stages, we often think of grief as a progression...like steps. Once we pass through one, we move on to the next and keep going. However, grief is not like that. It more often occurs in cycles. We cycle through different stages as we move through different phases in our life.

Thus, grieving isn't linear, and the stages of grief can overlap. We cycle through them at different times in our lives. The stages may occur in various orders each time. The experience of grief is highly individual and can look very different for each of us and with each experience of loss.

Early Life Loss

Losing a loved one early in life can look different than losing someone later. Society as a whole tends to minimize the impact of loss on kids.

Unfortunately, there are many myths about childhood grief. A common misperception is that young children don't remember it, so it doesn't matter. This belief is completely false.

Another mistake is that since children don't look like adults do, they must not be grieving. However, grief looks very different in children than it does in adulthood.

Regrettably, many believe that if a child doesn't cry or talk about it, they aren't being impacted by it in the same way that adults are and therefore grief for a child must not be as big of a deal. This belief is patently false.

Everyone experiences grief, but most adults don't understand how different grief is for children or how the impact of grief on children can be lifelong.

I can't tell you how often I've heard comments like, "Good thing she is so little; she won't remember it." Or, "At least the little one won't suffer as much; she's too little to understand what is going on."

But, unfortunately, both of these statements are wrong. Just because a child isn't old enough to speak doesn't mean they aren't old enough to sense the distress around them and to feel the loss of someone who had previously interacted with them.

Although uncommon, about 3.5% of children under 18 experience the death of a parent (Christ, 2000). Grief is experienced differently by children based on their age and developmental stage. The long-term effects of loss are also impacted by the time the child loses their mother. It is a myth that young children aren't affected by loss simply because they don't remember it or don't talk much about it.

Nothing is more unsettling to a child than the loss of a parent. Our survival depends on being cared for, provided for, and nurtured. As an infant, one doesn't recognize that the parent is a separate being. Infants cannot distinguish that Mom isn't just another part of their body like an additional arm. The ability to recognize separateness grows as a baby grows, but toddlers and young children don't yet know that others think and feel differently.

Toddlers and young children also view the world as if they (the child) make everything happen. These aren't conscious thoughts, and it is just how they understand the world. This phenomenon has nothing to do with intelligence or emotional maturity and is strictly due to brain development. The brain doesn't stop growing until we are around 25 years old, and the part of our brain that recognizes separateness is relatively underdeveloped early in life. Therefore, for infants and young children who lose a mother, that loss is like losing a part of themselves. It is highly distressing and creates a heightened sense of insecurity and fragility. The child's sense of safety is shattered.

Children under six struggle with the finality of death (Christ, 2010). They may appear to have limited emotional reactions, but that doesn't mean they aren't grieving.

Also, their ability to verbalize their experience is limited. This age group tends to have emotional outbursts sporadically.

Preschoolers also ask the same questions repeatedly because they struggle to understand the answers (Christ, 2010). Words like forever don't have a lot of meaning to a preschooler.

The baby book my mother kept for me includes a passage she wrote about how I struggled with understanding that my sister had died. She noted that I asked when Kim was coming home at least once a week despite being told that she had died, that Kim was in heaven, or that she was never coming home. As a mom myself, I now realize how painful that must have been for my mom. But, at the tender age of four, I didn't grasp it.

Younger children (under 10) experience magical thinking and are prone to inaccurately attribute cause-and-effect relationships to the loss (Christ, 2010). For example, a young child may have angry thoughts and wish that a parent would go away following an argument. Later, that parent unexpectedly dies. The child is at risk for believing their thought caused the parent to die somehow.

A child's grief experiences tend to intensify during developmental milestones. As a child understands the nature of loss, the experience of grief can strengthen. Periods of grief are also likely to increase during significant life events such as school transitions, dating, graduation, etc.

A child often appears to regress in their grief process rather than progress as they age. However, it's not regression; the child's cognitive and emotional capacities are growing. It isn't that they weren't able to grieve earlier. It is just that their ability to suffer as they age changes, and their grief process evolves as the child grows and matures.

When you observe a child after a loss, it looks like they grieve for short periods and then return to play as if nothing is wrong. They may appear unaffected or disinterested in the loss. (Christ, 2010).

One of my earliest memories is of the day we were on our way home from my older sister Kim's funeral. My younger sister Jennifer, who was days shy of three, and I (only four years old) were picked up at a family friend's house after the funeral. My dad was driving our old VW bug, my mother was in the passenger seat, and Jennifer and I were playing in the back seat. It was cold in the car, and I wanted to get home.

So, as was typical, I asked, "How is Kim?"

I remember the silence and then my mother stated, "She died, honey. She is in heaven now and won't be coming home anymore."

I clearly remember something was wrong, and I was supposed to be sad. So, we sat there quietly.

I remember thinking, "I wish we would get home soon; I want to play more."

I also remember as a teenager feeling guilty for this thought and many years of pain over what a horrible person I must have been for wanting to play after my sister died. Both my experiences as a child and teenager were completely normal. Sadly, I didn't understand it at the time.

At the ages of three and four, I didn't have the brain power to understand what was happening to my older sister. I heard words like cancer, sick, dying, heaven, and grief. But these words didn't mean a whole heck of a lot. However, I did understand that things weren't okay. I felt the sadness and fear of those around me. I knew what it meant when people around me cried.

I intuitively knew that life was difficult for my family. I knew my sister was in pain, and my parents didn't have time for me. I knew I could wake up in a stranger's home because something was going wrong. I became really good at sensing the emotional energy of those around me. This empathic attunement made it easier for me to be a "good girl." By feeling the needs of others, I became really good at helping them.

I may not have understood illness and death the way the adults did. I couldn't think about it or talk about it similarly. But the experience shaped my very personality. My brain developed in ways that strengthened my ability to emotionally read people.

But the early loss experience also taught me that I could lose people close to me. As a result, my overall sense of safety in the world was compromised. And thus, the foundations of anxiety were formed. My experience of childhood death was the loss of a sister, not my mother. Yet, the aftermath of that loss and the lasting impact it had on my mother has been part of shaping the person I am today.

Children can't think and talk about death. They aren't able to rationally make sense of what it means to be alive and what it means to be dead. Instead, children understand the world in concrete ways, focusing mainly on understanding their immediate experiences. None of these facts suggest that children aren't impacted by death. But it does mean that children don't have the same tools that adults have to understand and cope with the emotional intensity that follows death.

Lasting Impact

When your parent dies during childhood, your risk of adverse outcomes in adulthood increases. For example, there is an increased risk of mental health concerns such as anxiety, depression, suicidal behavior, and substance abuse (Nickerson et al., 2013). Physical symptoms and the ability to adaptively cope with adverse situations are also associated with the death of a parent during childhood (Luecken et al., 2009). As are educational attainment and career success, especially for those who lose a parent in early childhood (Nickerson et al., 2013).

Isabelle's mother died when she was 11 years old, and she reflected on how the grief process impacted her later in life.

She stated, "It seemed like forever. At different times in our lives. Weddings, children born, all the different things in life would create grief."

Although the experience of an early life loss has a lasting impact, the story isn't all bad. There are ways to minimize death's negative impact on a young person's later life. A child should experience as few changes after death as possible. Children must be given the space to grieve based on their developmental stage. Getting support for the child, as well as the wider family unit through counseling or psychotherapy, can make a huge impact in minimizing trouble later in life.

Later Life Loss

Grief doesn't just cycle and intensify during milestones for children. Adults experience this same pattern and you are likely to experience an increase in grief during life transitions. One of the significant developmental milestones for many women in adulthood includes the transition into motherhood. This transition has additional challenges for women who have lost their moms, regardless of what age they were when they lost her.

Leslie was eight months pregnant with her first child when her mother died.

She described her complicated grief process, "I didn't allow myself to grieve because my dad was in denial for a long time. I took the lead on things like the funeral. When my mom fell ill, I went to stay with her. I was living there and assumed many of her roles."

Leslie's story isn't an isolated one. Many adult daughters take on their mother's role in the family of origin. They take on the responsibility of taking care of everyone else and neglecting their own needs.

Grieving For What Was Lost

Have you had the experience of watching your child do something, and it makes you wonder if you did that same thing when you were that age? It is frustrating when that occurs, when you can't ask your mom about it. The ability to talk about our own experiences relating to our children with a loving mother is a loss that is rarely acknowledged. Unfortunately, that means we grieve alone.

Beth doesn't have many memories from her own childhood and when asked about what was difficult about being a mom without a mom, she stated, "Not being able to connect my childhood to my daughter. It's hard to know what I was like as a child because there wasn't anyone to ask. So, I am always searching for answers."

Grieving The Loss Of What You Wanted To Have

There is also the loss of what you wanted to have, a loving mother by your side. It doesn't matter if you had a great mom and she died, had a terrible mom, or never had a mom at all; we all wish we could get the support and guidance from a mom who knows and loves us.

If you are a mom who is estranged from your mother or you have an unhealthy or distant relationship, you know how complicated this grief can be. After all, it can be challenging to come to terms with the fact that you miss something you don't have or maybe even never had.

Each Grief Experience Is Unique

I was 27 years old and had lost my mother and both of my sisters. My father was in despair. I was alone and lost. Yet, the experience of grief for each loss was different. Kim died at the age of seven when I was four. My early childhood was filled with the tragedy of terminal leukemia and its impact on our family. Illness, death, and intense grief were the backdrops in which my personality was formed. Unsurprisingly, I grew up to be a psychologist who helps people heal from traumatic emotional wounds.

The death of my mother resulted in a feeling of intense vulnerability. Despite the difficulty we experienced during the last year of her life, my mom always felt like a safety net for me. I knew she loved me, and she was someone who would always be there. And now she was gone.

And then, Jennifer died. I hadn't realized how much my own identity was tied to being someone's sister. For the first time in my life, I wasn't anyone's sister. Jennifer and I were only 18 months apart. She was a massive part of my life, even though we were adults living in different states and leading very different lives. It felt like a literal piece of me had been ripped out.

It is essential to recognize that each grief experience is unique to you and that each loss is unique. There isn't anything wrong if your grief is different than what you expected. I want you to know that your grief process is valid, no matter what it looks or feels like.

Grieving As A Mom

One of the challenging aspects of grieving as a mom is that you still need to take care of your children. So, you are left juggling their needs (and their grief process if they are grieving) while you try to navigate your own experiences.

As Sophia said, "You don't have the opportunity to be how you are. You always have to have that happy and okay aura about you for your kids."

It is essential to give yourself permission to acknowledge and feel your grief. Although you may need to put on a happy face sometimes, it is okay if others, including your children, see your sadness. It is a normal human emotion, and seeing it won't damage your kids. Rather, it helps them build empathy.

REFERENCES

American Psychological Association. (2022). Grief. Retrieved December 10, 2022 from https://www.apa.org/topics/grief

Bergman, A., Axberg, U. & Hanson, E. (2017). When a parent dies – a systematic review of the effects of support programs for parentally bereaved children and their caregivers. *BMC Palliat Care, 16*, 39. https://doi.org/10.1186/s12904-017-0223-y

Christ, G. (2000). *Healing Children's Grief: Surviving a parent's death from cancer*. Oxford University Press.

Christ, G. (2010). Children bereaved by the death of a parent. In Corr, C. & Balk, D. *Children's encounters with death, bereavement, and coping*, 169-193. Springer Publishing Company.

Kübler-Ross, E. (1969). *On death and dying*. MacMillan.

Luecken, L., Kraft, A., Appelhans, B. & Enders, C. (2009). Emotional and cardiovascular sensitization to daily stress following childhood parental loss. *Developmental Psychology, 45(1)*, 296-302. doi:10.1037/A0013888.

Nickerson, A., Bryant, R., Aderka, I., Hinton, D, & Hofmann, S. (2013). The impacts of parental loss and adverse parenting on mental health: Findings from the National Comorbidity Survey-Replication. *Psychological Trauma: Theory, Research, Practice, and Policy, 5(2)*, 119-127. https://doi.org/10.1037/a0025695

O'Conner, M. (2022). *The Grieving Brain: The Surprising Science of How We Learn from Love and Loss*. HarperOne.

CHAPTER 5

THE TRANSFORMATIONAL POWER OF GRIEF

After a loss, grief is an emotion that we have throughout life. The intensity may vary, but it doesn't go away. That doesn't mean you are doomed to feel sad for the rest of your life. The grief process is not only healthy and normal, but also transformative.

Grief is something that many people fear. Many view it as a considerable burden, dangerous, or beyond their ability to manage.

I have often heard comments like, "You must be strong for...." as if showing our grief means we are weak.

As one who has experienced grief in many forms, I no longer fear it. I recognize the role it has played throughout my life. It is a familiar emotion, just as love, joy, excitement, and sadness are. I know that when I feel it, I am still okay. It will not overtake me or harm me, and the intensity of it will diminish.

Becoming comfortable with my grief was a long process. I spent the first 22 years of my life fearing it. Through therapy, I learned about the hold it had on my life and was able to make changes. I have been confronted with varying types of losses, including death, divorce, moves, miscarriages, and estrangement. While I don't like the feeling of grief, I know it, accept it, and no longer try to avoid it.

Everyone's grief process is unique, and yours will look different from mine. But I want you to know that you, too, can find growth and peace in grief.

Sophia's mom died four days after Sophia gave birth to her daughter, who was immediately admitted to the NICU. After that, she didn't feel like she could grieve because she needed to take care of her baby.

It's been eight years and Sophia said, "This year, I have started doing a lot of inner healing, trauma healing, and grief healing. I parent the way I would have wanted to be parented. If it doesn't align with my values, I don't do it."

Like Sophia, grief has helped me recognize my own resilience. I know that I can experience challenging things and remain the person that I am proud to be. Grief will neither devastate nor destroy me. Although it may slow things down, it does not have the power to derail my life.

Grief Healing Model

There are three parts to my grief healing model. I will describe them in order, but the process is cyclical, not stepwise. We cycle through them repeatedly in different aspects of our life.

When grief is triggered, we need to go through the process again. Fortunately, the more we cycle, the easier it becomes to go through the process and feel comfortable with our grief.

Remember, grief doesn't end; we become less distressed by it and, eventually, we can be at peace with it.

While grief is a natural part of life, and we don't need to hide it from others, it is possible to experience disordered grief. I define disordered grief as a process that results in an intense decline in functioning beyond what is typically experienced.

So, for example, grief that significantly impacts your daily life beyond the first year of loss is disordered. Clinical depression, prolonged (for more then three months) insomnia, significant vocational or educational mistakes, severe disruptions in relationships, and suicidal thoughts (beyond fleeting thoughts that are easily dismissed) are not normal parts of grieving.

Psychotherapy is a critical part of healing disordered grief. When it goes untreated, it can negatively impact you and your family.

For example, Chloe's mother was also without a mom, having lost her mom when she was 18. Chloe reports that her grandmother's death really impacted her mom and that she never recovered from it. Chloe's mom experienced disordered grief.

Chloe stated, "It always haunted my childhood. I've kept my mom's spirit alive for my daughter without projecting my grief onto her."

This can be a challenging but critical balance to achieve. The grief healing process I outline below can help you experience a healthy grief process that doesn't impair you or your family.

Recognize Grief

Leslie lost her mother just a couple of months before she gave birth to her first child.

She described the first several days postpartum as particularly difficult, "On day three, when my oldest was born, when my milk came in, I couldn't control my emotions. I felt very alone. I didn't have anyone to help, to stay with me. I had nothing. I felt like I had nobody to call. That is when I needed my mom the most."

Leslie's experience is what we often think about when we hear grief. However, grief can appear in subtle ways as well.

For example, I remember a time several years ago when my son Jackson was in Little League, and we were watching him play. Jackson was more of a mascot and cheerleader for the team than an athletic contributor, but he had a lot of heart.

I noticed my mood shift from enjoyment to a place of melancholy and irritability for no particular reason. My mind had begun to wander to conversations I imagined having with my mom, who had been my Little League coach. The mild feelings of sadness and unexplained irritability were actually unrecognized grief.

Grief can be tricky to identify. Sometimes, it's the punch-you-in-the-gut type of experience. But other times it can be subtle and sneak up on you.

It takes a little reflection for you to get comfortable with recognizing your grief. One of the ways you can identify it is by noticing where your mind wanders to.

- Are your thoughts returning to times in the past?
- Do you find yourself thinking about experiences you've had with your mom?
- Are you having imaginary conversations with her?

You may even notice yourself imagining things that never happened, but you wish could have happened.

Grief isn't a bad thing that we need to overcome. I don't try to avoid thinking about my mom. In fact, there are times when I enjoy those conversations in my head. However, it helps to recognize grief for what it is, so that if it negatively impacts my mood or behavior I can make changes as needed.

In the example above, I was no longer enjoying the game. Once I recognized that the grief was creating a negative impact, I acknowledged it and brought my full attention back to the game. Within a few moments, my enjoyment was back and all was right with my world.

I've created an easy-to-follow five-step guide you can follow to bring your attention back to what you are experiencing. You can find it at this link: Https://bit.ly/Enjoy-motherhood-guide.

Express Your Grief

I live in the Northeast of the United States and in this part of the world, most people are uncomfortable with other people's grief. Have you ever had an experience where you are talking about something sad, and someone will try to cheer you up or change the subject?

Unfortunately, many moms without a mom learn to keep their grief to themselves. They stop sharing their stories. And some eventually stop talking about their mother altogether.

But grief doesn't go away simply because we stop expressing it. In fact, when we stop expressing our suffering, it comes out in unintentional ways. It sneaks up on us. It comes out as irritability, short-temperedness, withdrawal, lethargy, shutting down, or conflicts in relationships.

So, how do you express your grief?

There are more ways to express grief than what people typically think. Talking with someone is just one way to express our emotions. The following examples are things that I have found helpful.

But remember, there are no wrong ways to express your sorrow. You can be as original or as creative as you'd like. The critical point is to take what you are experiencing inside your mind and/or body and somehow put it out in the universe.

Share Your Stories

Sharing your stories is so vital for the process of healing. What do I mean by sharing your stories? When we share memories of a past experience, we are telling a story.

Memories aren't tape recordings in your head that represent a stagnant reality of the event. Instead, memory is the recreation of sensory experiences that are influenced by your life experiences as well as your current mood state. When you share a memory, you recreate the past experience.

Because memories are recreations, you can influence the emotional impact memories have. You don't need to fear a memory, because a memory can't wound you. The memory may include painful emotional experiences, but you are safe and can redirect your awareness to more comfortable emotional experiences anytime.

Therefore, sharing your stories helps take the bitter edge off the memory. You can gain a sense of comfort with it and no longer need to rely on avoiding memories as a primary coping mechanism. The more you share your stories, the more comfortable you become with them.

You can share your past experiences verbally by talking with friends, family, or professionals such as counselors or coaches. You can also share your stories by writing them down in letters, journals, or memoirs.

Create Music

Music is a powerful way to evoke an emotional response which can be used to help you while you're grieving (O'Callaghan, 2013). As a mom, you use this tool naturally when you sing to your children. You intuitively recognize the soft power of a gentle lullaby to calm a fussy baby. You know a quick way to get your toddler moving by singing an upbeat, silly song. Speaking of silly songs, they can also make us laugh. And all of us have spent time crying to sad songs after a loss or a breakup.

I am a huge fan of making up my own songs. I am not a songwriter by any means. But I love creating pieces simply by singing the words in my heart. When my son was little, I loved to sing about how I loved him to the sun, moon, stars, and back. I would sing to him about how he was terrific. At 11, I still sing him a silly good morning song (and it still makes him smile as he opens his eyes).

I have found singing words from my heart related to my mom has been very powerful. No one hears these songs. They rarely are repeated, as I make them up each time. But each time is a powerful release of emotion. Sometimes that emotion is sadness, sometimes anger, and other times it's longing. It is whatever is in my heart at the time. There are no rules; I sing for as long as I feel like it. Sometimes, it's simply humming or whistling.

Singing recorded songs from your favorite artist is also helpful. You don't need to create your own songs for them to be meaningful. Emotion is evoked and released as we sing or move our bodies and toxins are released by our tears when we cry.

Listening to instrumental music (music without words) can also evoke and release emotion. The absence of words helps stimulate mental imagery, which can be very healing.

Move Your Body

Our body holds emotion. Many people recognize tension in their shoulders or neck. We also hold grief in our bodies (Mitchell, 2012). My body feels uncharacteristically heavy when I am experiencing grief. My lower back aches, and I get sharp muscle cramps in my thighs. I also am prone to a choking sensation when the distress is acute.

I have found that moving my body is a great way to release grief. Of course, periods of cardiovascular exercise such as running or dancing are helpful, but so are more gentle forms of movement such as stretching and Tai Chi.

Our bodies are designed to move rather than be sedentary. So, it makes sense that movement is a healthy release for grief. If you are feeling restless or agitated, move around a bit. This is what your body needs at the moment. I have learned to trust my body. I may not be fully aware of my emotional state at the time, but I can trust my body to let me know what it needs.

Be Creative/Artistic Expression

Artistic expression is a great way to release grief. The brain's emotional centers are more closely connected with the features of our brain that process images and music rather than language and reason. So, amazing things can happen if we let ourselves express an experience without thinking about it.

There is great healing power in expressing our grief through creating art. Examples include but are not limited to drawing, sketching, painting, sculpting, doodling, singing, songwriting, playing an instrument, creating poetry, writing, knitting, crocheting, pottery, and ceramics. The options are endless.

Here is a technique I like to use: I sit with a pencil in my hand and see what emerges. Sometimes, it's simple lines on paper. Sometimes, it is a sketch. Sometimes, I purposefully attempt to draw something that has come to my mind.

There is no right or wrong way to express grief through art. Let yourself release what comes forth in whatever manner feels right.

Speak Out Loud To Yourself

Trust me, there is a benefit to it. The act of vocalizing stimulates our vagus nerve, which has a prominent role in the body's calming response. When we speak out loud, we engage multiple parts of our brain — including the prefrontal cortex (thinking), motor centers, and limbic system (emotions). Furthermore, we also employ the hearing centers in our brains as we process the sounds of what has been spoken. When multiple brain centers are engaged, we can better process and thus release grief.

When we keep things in our heads, it is like trapping air in a balloon. The more we add, the more pressure builds up. As the pressure builds, the balloon becomes more fragile and vulnerable to popping. However, when we speak out loud, the air is released back into the atmosphere and the balloon is less fragile.

Also, when we speak things out loud, we are better able to hear things that we may not have noticed before. Thinking and listening are different. There can be a cathartic release when we say something versus when we believe it. And when we speak to ourselves, we can be open and honest without fearing criticism from others.

Writing

Writing is a powerful tool for releasing emotions. Whether taking pen to paper or typing in your favorite digital diary, writing can tap into and release emotions that may be buried deep down inside of you.

Why is writing so beneficial? Because it taps into multiple parts of the brain.

For example, writing requires using our thinking centers — which are part of the prefrontal cortex, the motor centers of the cortex, visual centers, and sensory centers. In addition, the limbic system, central to our experience of emotion, becomes interconnected with these other parts of the brain — which helps us more fully process our experiences. As you can see by now, amazing things happen when various parts of the brain are simultaneously called into action.

Journaling

Journaling is a common and valuable means of releasing emotions. You can journal using any paper or digital device. I like to make my journals special and typically have different ones for different purposes. That is my preference — but I recognize that for some, it may seem overly complicated and cumbersome. I have paper and pen journals and a journal app on my phone and tablet. I prefer paper journals without lines because I like having open space for sketching or doodling as I write.

I journal freely, which means I write what comes to mind at the time. Sometimes, it is just words. Sometimes, it is coherent thoughts. Sometimes, it is a conversation with myself.

Using journal prompts can be a helpful form of journaling as well. There are journals focused on particular topics or life experiences. Ultimately, you may find that a variety of journals meet your needs.

I invite you to find a journal that speaks to your heart. You are unique, and your thoughts and emotions belong in a fabulous container. I usually get myself a fun and special pen to use as well. Journaling is a special time for me, so the implements I use are also special.

Write Letters

One of my favorite ways to express grief is to write letters. I typically write these letters in a journal and have no intention of sending them to anyone. These are my private thoughts, emotions, and experiences. However, unlike journaling, there is an intended recipient when you write a letter. Directing your thoughts and feelings to someone is a potent way to release the energy pent up by the emotion related to that person.

For many years even before my mother died, I wrote her letters in my journal. Sometimes these were long explanations of why I was so angry with her, and other times they were heartfelt apologies for the pain we had caused each other. There were times when I did nothing but sling curses at my mother and times when I shared moments of weeping with her.

There were nights when I wrote, "I miss you." or "I wish you were here."

Sometimes, I would write, "I wish you could have known me better, and I wish you could have been healthier both physically and emotionally."

Over time, these letters became more conversational; I shared my experiences, fears, and hopes. When Jackson was born, I started sharing stories about him. I even started to ask questions in the letters. It began to feel like a conversation. The anger, bitterness, resentment, and despair I felt no longer choked me. The intensity of those feelings had faded. I now enjoy the time I spend thinking about my mother. I have never once reread them, and I never will.

I've written letters to others as well: my sisters, my father, friends, and God. It doesn't matter if the person I am writing to is alive or dead. These letters are for me, not for them.

Create Rituals

A ritual is a typical way of behaving. Rituals create a sense of safety and security. They help us recognize what is coming next, what is expected, and how to respond.

Each family has their own set of rituals. One of my childhood family rituals included a good night hug, kiss, and "I love you" to every family member before bed. This was just part of what we did for as long as I can remember. When I left for college and no longer saw or talked to my family members daily (this was before long-distance calling was free and texting was not yet a thing), I really missed it. After I settled into bed, I started saying it in my head and it became part of my nightly routine. It allowed me to still feel connected to them.

I still mentally run through a series of "I love you's" to each of my loved ones before bed, and I find comfort in it. I attend a "Blue Christmas" service each year that is provided expressly for those mourning during the holidays. Following this service allows me to think about my late loved ones and our past holidays together, and the sadness and grief are then released. It allows me to be more fully present during the remainder of the holiday season.

I invite you to incorporate rituals that bring peace and comfort. There is no right or wrong when it comes to creating practices. Make them as simple, creative, and elaborate as feels helpful to you.

Spiritual Practices

Many people find comfort in spiritual beliefs and/or religious practices when they are faced with times of grief or other hardships. However, for others, it is during these difficult times that they find themselves pulling away from their previously held beliefs. I have done both at different times in my life. As an adolescent and young adult, I felt angry and separated from God. Conversely, for most of my adult life, especially after giving birth to my son, I have been drawn to the mysteries of my faith and the comfort it provides.

I have found comfort in prayer, scripture reading, and faith-based music during times when my grief is uncomfortable. Talking with members of my faith community has also been extremely helpful during periods of intense grief or mourning. Walking a prayer labyrinth and spending time in silence have also been healing.

Fill In The Relationship Gaps

My mother and I had a major argument eight months before she died, which led to an estrangement. We both were hurting and said things we shouldn't have. We went eight months without speaking.

The week before she died unexpectedly, I was offered an interview for a post-doctoral residency. I called home to tell my dad about it and my mother answered the phone. I quickly gave her the news and she said she was happy to hear it and was proud of me. She then quickly gave the phone to my father. That was the last conversation we ever had.

I was very angry with my mother during our estrangement. My anger fueled my continued separation from her and, at times, masked my sadness over no longer having her in my life. One of my favorite things about our relationship was how much I loved talking to her about my successes. She was always so proud of me, and I realize now how much she vicariously lived through me. But, unfortunately, it felt like a burden at the time.

Nevertheless, I loved calling her anytime, day or night, simply saying, "Guess what I did?" and hearing the joy in her voice as she tried to guess. It didn't matter how big or small my news was; in that instant, she was excited. That is all that mattered to either of us.

When we became estranged, and after she died, I no longer had that. Calling my dad wasn't the same. He didn't have the same excitement that my mother had. Friends had their own lives, and it wasn't as exciting to them.

This is just one example of the many gaps left when my relationship with my mom was no longer close.

What Is A Relationship Gap?

Relationships are an integral part of our human experience. We are meant to live in relationship with others. Everyone has unique talents, strengths, interests, and passions. The people we choose to spend time with have qualities that are compatible with ours. That isn't to say that our interests and passions are the same; instead, there is harmony among them.

When we lose a relationship or the connection is dramatically altered, we experience a Relationship Gap. Each person adds something to our life or fills a need, whether it is emotional support, a shared history, providing information or assistance, or someone to do things with. When a person's role in our life is altered, what they provide is no longer available, and thus a Relationship Gap is left.

The Relationship Gap adds another dimension to the grief we experience. Not only do we grieve the loss of the person in our life, but we also miss what the person added to our life. For example, when I lost my mother, I no longer had the person I shared my joys with.

Although we can never replace the person we lost, we can fill the Relationship Gaps. This, of course, takes time. After the acute stages of grief, we notice that the Relationship Gaps and fresh waves of grief emerge. Over time, as the grief's intensity diminishes, we can begin to reflect on the Relationship Gaps and how we can fill them.

Filling Relationship Gaps is not a betrayal. No one can ever replace the absence of the person you lost, and no one can ever replace a mother. However, we are meant to live in relationship with others. We are not destined to live the remainder of our lives with huge gaps. Therefore, creating new connections or altering existing relationships is appropriate to minimize the negative impact of Relationship Gaps.

Gaps To Be Filled

There are five common relationship gaps that moms experience when they lose their mother or don't have a healthy relationship. Your mom may have filled some or all of these functions. However, it is crucial to recognize that most people who aren't our mothers don't naturally fill more than one or two roles in our lives — which is okay. I will talk more about this in the following chapters.

I recognize that no one person or combination of people will ever completely fill the gaps left by our mothers. I am not suggesting that our mothers are replaceable. But instead, by filling in some of the holes, we can feel higher levels of comfort and contentment. I will always miss my mother. Fortunately, the intense pain of grief isn't triggered as often.

I still feel the loss, but it isn't as distracting to my present experience. It is much easier now to stay fully present in the daily moments of joy. Of course, I would have preferred my mother to still be in my life — but I am glad I have found ways to get support, comfort, assistance, and joy from other places.

Shared History

Most of us have a shared history with our mothers that is unique to that relationship. Often, they are the ones that can share the most details about our childhood along with the heartwarming and embarrassing stories about us. They can tell us things about ourselves that we didn't know or weren't as familiar with.

Sometimes, we can partially fill this gap with our relationships with other family members such as other parents or parent figures, siblings, aunts, uncles, grandparents, or cousins. For example, my relationship with my father changed after my mother died. We had always been close, but I began relying on him to share the inside family jokes and stories. I also found myself bonding with my aunt, who is 10 years older than I am. She remembers a lot of my early life and has been able to laugh with me about those early days.

You may even have a long-standing friendship that fills this gap. Sometimes, friends can fill in those memories in ways that even our family isn't privy to. They also know us in unique ways that we can find comfort in.

Emotional Support

One of the most common Relationship Gaps that moms without a mom experience is emotional support. Typically, our mother is the first to soothe and care for us after birth. A woman's body releases oxytocin when giving birth, which enhances her ability to bond with her new infant. For many of us, we continue to receive emotional support far into our adulthoods.

Even those women who have a strained or estranged relationship with their mothers wish they could go to her for support, even knowing it wouldn't be given. Most women describe giving love and support to their children as one of the most essential roles of a mother. So when we don't have it, either because we lost it or if we never had it, the desire for it leaves a Relationship Gap.

Not everyone is skilled at providing emotional support. Intense emotion, especially grief, is something that many people try to avoid. Genuine emotional support comes from simply listening without judgment. An excellent emotional listener can sit with your emotion without needing to cheer you up or give advice. Instead, they sit with you no matter what emotion you are expressing.

Most of us want to be good emotional supporters. Unfortunately, in our desire for people to feel better, we are quick to offer distraction or advice. Neither feels good to the person who wants to be heard.

Be direct with the people you go to for support and let them know what you need. If you don't get what you need, ask them to listen.

If they start giving advice, it is appropriate to say something like, "I appreciate your suggestion, but right now, what would be most helpful is for you to listen. You don't need to make it better for me."

It may take several instances of using this technique before you notice any change. After several tries, if the person is still not able to listen in a way that is supportive, take note of this and recognize that even though they are well-intentioned, they aren't able to fill this Relationship Gap. They can still be a great friend, but not an excellent emotional supporter.

Information

I remember coming home from the hospital after giving birth to Jackson and being frightened to go to the bathroom. I had stitches and bleeding and had been given instructions about what to do to keep the area clean. But I couldn't remember which bottle of liquid was used first, what was used after, and where to apply creams. Not only was I dreading doing something wrong with my son, but I also couldn't even pee without feeling like I was going to mess something up. I had no one to ask; this wasn't something I wanted to talk with my friends about, even though they would have been more than happy to help.

Most moms without a mom I've spoken with wished they had a mom to ask questions to and who could teach them about how to take care of a baby and how to be a mom. Unfortunately, we are not born knowing how to be a mom.

Humans learn through experience, by what is modeled for them, and by asking questions. The natural person to turn to for things related to mothering is, of course, our own mother. However, if she is not actively in our lives, it is vital to get this information elsewhere.

I recommend getting information from trusted people in your life. This can include other family members, friends, and professionals such as teachers, childcare workers, coaches, therapists, ministers, or psychologists. Although we can get a lot of great information through technology nowadays, it can be challenging to discern what is helpful to our situation (and, frankly, if we can even trust it).

Assistance

Like all new mothers, I was completely sleep deprived those first few months after giving birth to my son. Neither my husband nor I have family that live near us. I had just moved to the town a year earlier and as a shy introvert, I hadn't yet made close friends. There wasn't anyone I could ask to give me time for a nap. However, I have learned that asking for help when I need it (or even want it) is appropriate. I will talk more about this later in the book.

For most people, moms are the go-to person when you need help. As young children, we run to Mommy when anything goes wrong or we can't do something alone. This tendency continues once we become mothers ourselves. Unfortunately, if our mom isn't available, we need help elsewhere.

You will hear me say this several times; it is that important. We are only physically designed to manage *some* of our family's needs. Humans are social animals; it truly takes a community to raise children. So, there is no shame in asking for help.

Activity Partner

Playing on a playground was difficult for Jackson when he was young due to his neurological disorders. Navigating the equipment was scary for him and we spent a lot of time in physical therapy building his safety and confidence in his body, so he could freely play like the other children.

One of the things I missed during that time was having my mom go to the playground with me. I wanted her to celebrate Jackson's wins just like I did. I wanted her to ask about his progress. I wanted her to join us for his activities.

Once I intentionally tried to fill this Relationship Gap, there was a huge emotional boost. I started inviting other family members and friends to many of Jackson's things, and I was surprised by how many things people said yes to and how it enhanced my relationships.

We expect grandmothers to take a considerable interest in our children, second only to us. When this isn't the case, many moms without a mom miss having a mother to share the fun and challenging things with us. Although we may be uncomfortable inviting other people into our children's lives, once we do, it can be hugely rewarding — for our children as well as for ourselves.

REFERENCES

O'Callaghan, C., McDermott, F., Hudson, P. & Zalcberg, J. (2013). Sound continuing bonds with the deceased: The relevance of music, including Preloss Music Therapy, for eight bereaved caregivers. *Death Studies, 37,* 101-125.

Mitchell, D. (2012). Moving and breathing through grief. In Neimeyer, R., *Techniques of Grief Therapy,* 67-79. Routledge.

Near, R. (2012). Intermodal expressive arts. In Neimeyer, R., *Techniques of Grief Therapy,* 67-79. Routledge.

CHAPTER 6

THE ROLE A MOM PLAYS IN OUR LIFE

Growing up, my mother played many roles. Although she worked outside the home, she made sure my sister and I had the opportunity to participate in any available activity. I became a Girl Scout Brownie; thus, my mom became one of the leaders. I began playing Little League softball, so my mother became one of the coaches. She attended all my games, band concerts, chorus recitals, dance recitals, and anything else I was involved in.

As a child, my mother was my supporter, cheerleader, chauffeur, activity manager, and household director. Although my sister Jennifer and I were responsible for the maintenance of the home at a very young age, it was my mother who oversaw it all. She kept track of everything. And if we needed help with something, she provided it. When we got hurt, she took care of us. She handled everything. Or so it seemed at the time. I learned much later what it actually was like for her as well as for us. More about that later.

I grew up with the notion that moms did everything. After all, my mother worked, cared for us, was a community leader, taught others, kept us safe, healed our wounds, kissed us goodnight, and was well respected. I didn't realize at the time the colossal toll this took on her. She died at 51 years old from congestive heart failure, the complications of diabetes, and years of pain from a degenerative back condition. Her mental health dramatically impacted her physical health. She paid a huge price for being everything to everyone and leaving nothing for herself.

Motherhood and female identity has been intertwined throughout history (Medina & Magnuson, 2009; Chodorow, 1990; McMahon, 1995; Glenn, 1994). Before I became a mom at 37, I was often mistaken for being a mother. We see adult women and automatically assume they are a mom.

Women today must juggle self-care, work, friendships, intimate relationships, and motherhood. We view mothers as capable of managing all these roles while prioritizing their children. Our expectation of what makes a good mother has become so challenging and complex that most mothers today view themselves as falling short somehow (Medina & Magnuson, 2009).

Despite what society tells us, we are not biologically designed to provide all of the needs for our family on our own. The human species is made to live in a community. We, as mothers, have been raising our children with the assistance of family, friends, and other community members. This is the way that humans have developed since the beginning of time.

Unfortunately, with the advent of the nuclear family over the past century and the normalization of children moving away from their family of origin, Western culture has increasingly promoted the idea that each distinct family unit should be completely self-sufficient. Unfortunately, this notion has been particularly detrimental to women. The risk of depression, suicide, and substance abuse rises when families are cut off from extended family and community support (Vandenberg-Daves, 2014).

Many moms believe they should be able to care for their families independently. Regrettably, this is an impossible task. Mothers can't fulfill every role or responsibility. We just can't!

Mothers provide for the physical needs of our children. When our children are infants, this includes the energy-intensive process of nursing our child, whether that be through breastfeeding or bottle feeding. In addition, we provide a safe environment in which they develop.

Nervous system development is impacted by the child's environment in the early years of life. As the brain develops, the child becomes increasingly independent in daily activities such as sleeping, toileting, feeding, and communicating. This increased independence doesn't mean a decline in care for moms, but rather a change in how they care.

As children grow, moms often continue in our role as primary caregivers. Examples of typical responsibilities include:

- Providing meals.
- Cleaning the house.
- Helping with homework.
- Volunteering at school functions.
- Providing transportation to activities.
- Assisting children in navigating peer relationships.

Mothers are the first people children ask for advice or emotional support. When they don't feel well, children often look for their mom first. If they don't know how to do something, it is their mom who they seek out. If they have a bad dream, they wake Mom up in the middle of the night to make it all better.

A sense of safety in the world begins to develop during infancy and is primarily influenced by the mother-infant relationship. In healthy relationships, moms help children feel secure, allowing them to take healthy risks and explore their world.

Conversely, moms who don't have a safe bond with their mother often experience a decline in the feeling of security. This insecurity carries over into our own motherhood and can manifest itself subtly as grief.

For example, Beth's mother died when she was 21 years old. Beth had her child at 39 and, like me, she was surprised by the intensity of grief she felt when she became a mom. Beth found that her sense of security had been shaken.

She stated, "I am super always in her business. I am always hyper focused. If she coughs and I'm like, 'Are you okay?' She will fall down, and I will go to the worst-case scenario. I'm more hands-on and very protective of her. Not a helicopter parent, but hyper aware and sensitive to her. I think I probably gave in to her needs more than my mom did to me. I'm like, 'Let's do it; you only live once.' I'm trying to be more present."

Mothers take care of us when we are children. As we grow, we become more independent, and our reliance on our mother's care decreases. This doesn't mean that as we enter adulthood, we no longer benefit from the wisdom and guidance of our mothers. We can always benefit from being open to the insights of the older generations, especially our mothers.

Women are not born with the knowledge of how to care for and raise children. We learn this through the support, guidance, and modeling of those around us. For most women, having access to a supportive mother is invaluable. Moms tend to be the "go-to" for their daughters as they enter motherhood. A mom can provide her daughter with physical assistance when she needs it. She can provide emotional support and guidance. A mother shares her knowledge and experience with her daughter. And a mom is someone we can ask questions about anything. Unfortunately, the absence of a loving mom growing up creates a sense of insecurity and anxiety that can last into adulthood if not addressed.

Like when we are children, we continue to look toward a mother for support and guidance. It is natural to seek out one's mother because that has been the typical way of things throughout childhood and adolescence, even if you didn't have a mom.

So, what happens when we don't have our mother as a go-to person?

We must intentionally create a community of support and guidance. The following chapters will focus on who should be in that community as well as how to go about building it.

REFERENCES

Chodorow, N. (1990). Gender, relation, and difference in psychoanalytic perspective. In C. Zanardi (Ed.), *Essential papers on the psychology of women*, 420-436. New York University Press.

Glenn, E. (1994). Social constructions of mothering: A thematic overview. In E. Glenn, G. Chang & L. Forcey (Eds.), *Mothering: Ideology, experience, and agency*, 1-29. Routledge.

McMahon, M. (1995). *Engendering motherhood: Identity and self-transformation in women's lives.* Guilford Press.

Medina, S. & Magnuson, S. (2009). Motherhood in the 21st century: implications for counselors. *Journal of Counseling and Development, 87(1),* 90+.

Vandenberg-Daves, J. (2014). *Modern Motherhood: An American History.* Rutgers University Press.

CHAPTER 7

WHO WE NEED IN OUR COMMUNITY

One of the most challenging aspects of being a mom without a mom is the absence of that go-to person. Most women who have a loving and supportive mother can count on their mothers for assistance in myriad physical, emotional, and sometimes financial ways. For those moms without a mom, we need to get that assistance from others.

Four Important People In Our Mom Community

When creating our Mom Community, there are four people that every mom (especially moms without a mom) should have in her life. These people can include friends, family members, work friends, and professionals such as counselors, psychologists, coaches, and teachers. Your mom community may change over time, which is normal and okay. People come in and out of our lives for various reasons, but that does not diminish their importance.

The Wise Woman

I breastfed Jackson when he was with me and pumped breast milk to be used when I was not with him. Each day I provided the Early Learning Center, where he attended with a supply of breast milk and bottles for that day. One day when he was about six months old, I was dropping him off when the lead teacher in his room approached me.

She asked, "Melissa, do you think Jackson is ready to go up a nipple size?"

I looked at her as my jaw dropped. I had no idea what she was talking about. Literally, I had no clue. My mind was blank, and I felt my face getting hot.

At that point, all I could say was, "What?"

She saw my distress and very professionally explained that the holes in a bottle's nipple come in different sizes. Newborns and young infants require small nipple holes, so that the milk flow is slow and easily managed. As they grow, they can ingest more significant amounts of liquid and thus the nipple hole size increases. My son was taking a long time to feed and seemed to struggle. His teacher believed it was time to go up one nipple size.

I thanked her for the information and asked further questions about numbering and how to go about buying different sizes. The last thing I wanted to do was go into the store and feel as clueless and dumb as I did then.

I will never forget the intense shame I felt as I walked out of Jackson's classroom that day. I felt like I had just been given information that every other mother must have known. The fact that I had no idea about nipple sizes or the fact that my son was struggling felt like a dirty little secret I was ashamed of. I feared that the teacher now believed I was an incompetent fraud who was clueless about being a mom. I cried for most of the ride to work, repeatedly replaying that moment.

There wasn't something wrong with me because I didn't know something. After all, there was no one in my life who would have told me. There are lots of things we don't know until we are exposed to them.

We all need a Wise Woman in our community. A Wise Woman has had various life experiences, has a lot of knowledge, and generously shares what she knows. And if she doesn't have an answer, she knows where to get it. In addition, she is comfortable advising and offering suggestions when asked.

I have had many Wise Women in my life, but, unfortunately, there were many times I didn't seek them out and thus went on struggling. Part of my struggle is the fear of appearing incompetent or, dare I say it, stupid. It has taken me years to recognize how ingrained this tendency is and how often it gets in my way. But as I continue to walk down my path of personal growth, I've found that Wise Women are so incredibly generous with their knowledge and never (in my experience, anyway) look down on those whom they assist.

The Emotional Supporter

Eight months before my mother died, we had a major falling out. I was 24, completing my pre-doctoral internship in Pennsylvania, and living with my fiancé Tom. My mother had suffered from chronic illness, including degenerative disc disease, poorly controlled diabetes, and depression. In short, my mom was suffering and I didn't have the insight to understand or relate to her experience. Instead, I saw all of her actions that contributed to her suffering and I resented how her pain impacted my life.

My parents came to visit me in October 1998. Tom (my fiancé) and I were non-smokers who didn't allow smoking in our small one-bedroom apartment, so my parents chose to stay in a local hotel. My mother was a chain smoker and it was still legal to smoke in designated hotel rooms.

The visit was uncomfortable. My mom was in a lot of pain and she was constantly smoking, which, for some reason, I found intolerable despite the fact my mother had smoked my entire life. My parents spent very little time at our apartment because of our smoking prohibition, and the room in the hotel felt unbreathable to me because the smoke fog was so intense. On the last day of our visit, we went sightseeing. I was driving, my mother was in the passenger seat smoking, and I just wanted to get home to get out of the car. She moaned in pain with every bump, which I found annoying, and she felt that I could have been taking more care to avoid the bumps.

It was at this point that I unleashed on her about how she was hurting herself by the choices she was making in life and that I didn't want to be part of it. I wasn't kind; in fact, I was mean. Not surprisingly, she was defensive and mean right back. There was a lot of unconscious stuff that was getting churned up for both of us, but neither of us had the ability to address any of it in a healthy way. It was a horrible experience that sparked eight months of us not talking.

In June 1999, my internship ended and I was in the process of securing a residency. I was excited about it and wanted to share it with both my parents. Although my mother and I weren't speaking, my father and I were. When I called and my mother answered, she would normally just hand the phone over to my father without saying anything. But this time, when she answered, she listened to my news with happiness and kindness. It was just a few brief sentences, but it felt like a start. We didn't broach our relationship at all. Unfortunately, the next call I received was from my father, informing me that my mother had unexpectedly died.

Needless to say, I had a lot of emotion surrounding my relationship with my mother. It was very difficult to find someone who could listen to my pain without trying to change the subject or cheer me up. Thankfully, two people in my life knew the circumstances and were there to listen.

First, my best friend and former college roommate Lorin knew me well enough to know that there was more going on inside me than I let out. So, in those infrequent times when I would open up emotionally, she was unconditionally there to listen.

The other person I had was my Aunt Sandra. She knew both my mother and me and understood many of the dynamics without me needing to explain them. Both of these women were a Godsend to me and I will be forever grateful!

Given that emotional support is critical for good mental health, the second person we need in our Mom Community is an Emotional Supporter. An Emotional Supporter is a fantastic listener. She will let you pour your heart out, no matter the emotion. She won't try to cheer you up or give advice. She just listens. We live in a time when success and action are valued. However, we are more than what we do; we exist and we feel, and expressing ourselves is so vital to our emotional health.

As humans, we have what are called mirror neurons. These specialized cells in our brains allow us to turn what we observe into knowledge. In addition, mirror neurons foster imitation, laying the groundwork for understanding the experiences of others and promoting empathy (Rajmohan & Mohandas, 2007; Enticott et al., 2008). In other words, we are biologically hardwired to respond to the emotional experiences of those around us.

Humans experience emotion at different levels of intensity. There is a usual emotional ebb and flow within our day-to-day lives. There are variations in both the emotions we feel comfortable with such as joy, happiness, excitement, and love as well as those emotions we find distressing, such as sadness, fear, loneliness, and anger.

When uncomfortable emotions are intense, our body may interpret this as distress. We sense and react to the intense feelings that people around us are having thanks to our mirror neurons. While this is normal and healthy, many people are uncomfortable with intense emotion and thus automatically attempt to soothe, alter, or avoid it. We have all had the unsatisfying experience of sharing our feelings with someone to have them make a quick remark about how "it could be worse," "it will get better," "don't worry," or "it will be okay." These people aren't intentionally trying to dismiss us. Their nervous system is simply directing them away from the discomfort they feel from our emotions.

An Emotional Supporter is a person who is comfortable with intense emotions and can keep their nervous systems regulated and calm while their emotions are elevated. It feels incredible to share your inner world with someone who can sit comfortably alongside you. Furthermore, sharing the experience with someone helps the emotion fade naturally. When we share a safe space with a safe person, our body releases tension and lets go of stress.

The Go-Getter

I like to call the third person in our Mom Community, The Go-Getter. This is the person who knows how to get things done. We all know someone like this. They don't typically sit still; they are always doing something. These are the people that have completed 30 things by 8 am. They have a natural rhythm that lends itself to activity and enjoy being active and ticking things off a to-do list.

The Go-Getter is the friend to call on when you are over-whelmed with life's chores and things feel like they are piling up beyond your ability to manage. So, for example, I have a friend who will periodically come over to my house and do my sons' laun-dry for me. That simple little task is huge on several levels. Not only does it take one thing off my plate, but it's also a reminder that I am not alone in caring for my kids.

The emotional boost that we get from having someone help us is another benefit beyond completing the original task. As moms without a mom, we carry an additional burden of needing to ask, whereas, many mothers just know what their daughter needs. Over time, this drain impacts us through fatigue, irritability, and withdrawal.

There have been times when I felt terrible about myself because I wasn't as skillful at getting things done as some other moms were. It is essential to recognize that high energy, task-oriented, goal-driven, and efficiency are a subset of many personality char-acteristics. Each of us has our own unique set of features and traits that make up our personality. One isn't better than the other, and the fact that my personality doesn't include the gift of getting things done quickly and easily doesn't diminish my value as a mother.

Examples of what I call the "go-getter" can be found in descriptions of two of the "doer" types within the Myers-Briggs Personality types (Randall et al., 2017). The first is the Sensitive doers who "are very caring, generous, and always willing to help" (*Sensitive doer (ISFP)d*. Personality Type Center: The Sensitive Doer (ISFP), n.d.). The second type is the Laid-Back Doers, who "have no problem handling several tasks at once and to blossom out in crises" (*Laid-back doer (ESFP)*. Personality Type Center: The Laid-back Doer (ESFP), n.d.). People who fall into either of these personality types can be relied upon as "go-getters" within our community.

The Late-Night Talker

The fourth person that every mom without a mom should include in her Mom Community is the woman I call the Late-Night Talker. This is someone who always tends to be awake and makes herself available when we need her. Every mom who has had late-night feedings or had to soothe a baby whose sleep pattern was incongruent with the typical day/night schedule knows how easily one can become overwhelmed and need a little friendly boost.

Thankfully, it is becoming easier to find this person nowadays as our social connections are becoming more global. Therefore, a simple text chat via cell, messenger, or another social media platform can help a mom feel less alone in the overwhelming exhaustion and uncertainty that becomes more prevalent at night.

These conversations don't need to be in-depth or profound to be comforting. And yet, the intimacy created late at night has the potential to propel these casual interactions into meaningful friendships.

There may be times when a mom really needs the assistance or support of someone at night, and they cannot connect with any friends or family. At this point, it is essential to remember and use one of the available hotlines.

- 988 Suicide and Crisis Lifeline (formerly The National (USA) Suicide Prevention Lifeline): call 988 from anywhere in the USA or chat with them online at https://988lifeline.org/

- National (USA) Crisis Text Line: Text HOME to
  741741 from anywhere in the USA, anytime, about
  any crisis.

No matter who you reach out to, if you are struggling, please reach out. Every mom has been in that place, and I have yet to meet a woman who is angry or upset when a friend reaches out for help — even late at night.

Members of Our Community May Change Over Time

Our community is not set in stone. Friendships and professional relationships change over time. This is normal. People come into our lives, sometimes for specific reasons. However, every relationship is valuable, no matter how long or short the time together is.

Despite what we see in the media and society's expectations, we shouldn't raise our children alone. Both moms and children thrive when moms support moms. Having a solid community of mom friends you can rely on isn't only helpful, it is essential.

REFERENCES

Enticott, P., Johnston, P., Herring, S., Hoy, K. & Fitzgerald, P. (2008). Mirror neuron activation is associated with facial emotion processing. *Neuropsychologia, 46(11)*, 2851-2854.

Laid-back doer (ESFP). Personality Type Center: The Laid-back Doer (ESFP). (n.d.). Retrieved January 22, 2023 from https://www.personality-type.net/laid-back-doer/

Rajmohan, V. & Mohandas, E. (2007). Mirror neuron system. *Indian journal of psychiatry, 49(1)*, 66-69. https://doi.org/10.4103/0019-5545.31522

Randall, K., Isaacson, M. & Ciro, C. (2017). Validity and Reliability of the Myers-Briggs Personality Type Indicator: A Systematic Review and Meta-analysis. *Journal of Best Practices in Health Professions Diversity, 10(1)*, 1-27. Retrieved January 22, 2023 from https://www.jstor.org/stable/26554264

Sensitive doer (ISFP)d. Personality Type Center: The Sensitive Doer (ISFP). (n.d.). Retrieved January 22, 2023 from https://www.personality-type.net/sensitive-doer/

CHAPTER 8

HOW TO CREATE A MOM COMMUNITY

I have always been a shy introvert. I was the kid who would hide between my mother's legs when someone came to our house. I've never had a large group of close friends. Most of the time, I was befriended by the friends of whomever I was dating at any given time.

I was lucky to meet my best friend Lorin on my first day of summer college registration. Our rooms were across the hall from each other. At lunchtime, we walked out simultaneously, started chatting, and hit it off. We spent the rest of the weekend together and decided to be roommates during our first year. This was the best decision, as she became my best friend throughout college and remained one of my closest friends despite living in different states since graduation. Unfortunately, I hung out with my college boyfriend's group of friends and thus didn't create a strong network of friends myself beyond Lorin.

I have always struggled with making friends. This stayed the same once I became a mom. Although I have excellent social skills, I have never felt comfortable with small talk or being social in larger groups. My clinical practice kept me from becoming involved with any Mommy and Me groups that met during the day.

As my son Jackson grew, I began to notice he was not developing at the expected rate. Both his speech and motor development were delayed. As it turned out, after a full year of seeking out specialists and getting all kinds of testing done, we finally got the diagnosis of Childhood Apraxia of speech. My son was different from other people's children. My experience of being a mom was different. I felt even more alone.

My heart ached that his life was more challenging than most other children his age. I had no idea how I would juggle his physical therapy, occupational therapy, and speech therapy, all without the assistance of my mom. Fortunately, I was blessed to have my Aunt Sandra and my father to lean on during this process. I could talk with both of them about my fears and frustrations without feeling judged. They could listen to my pain without trying to change the subject or trying to cheer me up with invalidating optimism.

I remember the fears and sadness surrounding Jackson's struggles and eventual Apraxia diagnosis, which brought with it the real possibility that he would not be able to talk or even say his own name by the time he started school. There were fears that his physical challenges would make navigating the school environment difficult or that he would not be able to play with his peers in a meaningful way. Sleepless nights, countless evaluations, specialists, early intervention teachers, Individual Education Plan meetings, and hundreds of hours of physical, occupational, and speech therapy had been our usual way of life. For about two years, he had eight therapy sessions a week.

Through the grace of God, my son persevered, persisted, and thrived. My little guy never gave up and surpassed the expectations we were given. Instead, he taught me the strength and resilience of the human spirit. My son never ceased to amaze me, and I was humbled to have been given the honor of being his mother.

Church Community

After feeling alone for years, I finally found my community. I was raised Catholic and felt comfortable within that faith denomination. When my husband Tom and I married, he was attending the Lutheran church. He felt uncomfortable attending the Catholic church despite being an active churchgoer because he was divorced. I began attending with him and his three-year-old son Tommy and was pleased with how similar the services are, and I was pleasantly surprised to find that the theological beliefs of the Lutheran church resonated with me.

Early in our marriage, I had not yet decided to withdraw from Catholicism and become a Lutheran. I longed to talk with my mother about this since she and my father were from different faith traditions. She was Episcopalian and agreed to raise us Catholic so that the Catholic church recognized the marriage, which was important to my father.

Growing up, we went through Sunday school and mostly attended the Catholic church, but on holidays we went with my mother and my grandmother to the Episcopal church. My mother had considered converting to Catholicism at several points in her life, but decided not to. I wish we had talked about what it was like to be in a different denomination from us and what was behind her choices. It would have been lovely to share my thoughts, fears, and questions with her.

Attending church and being part of the community was difficult for the first several years of Jackson's life. I didn't feel comfortable leaving him in the church nursery, as he had already spent several days in the Early Learning Center while I worked. So, here was another area of our life where I felt inadequate and alone.

I was doing a lousy job incorporating faith into my son's life. And, of course, with that belief came a sense of shame. Yet again, I was failing.

And then, three things happened that significantly impacted my life.

1. Jackson entered kindergarten, and his outpatient therapy decreased to one night a week. I felt like he was thriving for the first time in years.

2. Before being a mom, I was the type who wouldn't just join something; I would lead it. Although I am pretty shy and creating friendships is difficult, I am comfortable taking on leadership positions. That doesn't feel personal, and I feel confident in the role. Unfortunately, once my son was born, my world shrank. All of my energy was going to keep my head above water. Every day was a struggle.

   Once Jackson entered kindergarten and his therapies decreased, my life became more manageable. At this point, I realized I needed to get back to being involved in things. I allowed myself to pursue leadership positions within the church and its Early Learning Center. I became a member, then a vice president, of the guidance committee, the governing body for his Early Learning Center, and was elected to the church council. As part of my church council role, I became involved with the mission and outreach committee. These positions allowed me new opportunities to meet people within the church and to develop meaningful relationships.

3. The third significant factor was a change in the church leadership, which included hiring a children's minister named Deacon Emily. After a month or two of her being in her new role, I invited Deacon Emily to breakfast. At this meeting, I shared my feelings that I wasn't doing a good job teaching our faith to my son. She was so gracious in listening to and supporting me. She offered me several easy things to try and, most importantly, she normalized my struggle.

The combination of these three events allowed me to create solid and lasting relationships. I began teaching an adult Sunday school class for parents of children who were infants, toddlers, or in elementary school. Since fostering faith within my family had been such a challenging experience for me, I wanted to help other parents struggling with similar experiences. It took about three years for the class to reach a consistent membership. But once it did, we became very close.

This group of about 16 other parents began sharing their faith stories, vulnerabilities, and personal stories. We became a close-knit group of support and friendship for each other. Through this group and the larger church community, I have found many of the members of my Mom Community.

It took several years, but I am now surrounded by people that I can count on. My community includes members of all four categories I talked about above. I no longer feel alone.

Where to Find Your Mom Community

Now that we know who to put in our Mom Community, we need to know where to find them. Members of our community can come from a variety of places. There is no right or wrong in this effort. Friendships can germinate in a variety of unexpected places.

Connecting with childhood friends who may live locally is a great place to start. Of course, staying connected with old friends who now live far away through social media isn't the same as having local friends, but many moms have found this helpful nonetheless.

It is common for relationships with family, both immediate and distant, to change once a new baby is born. However, you may find old relationships strengthening or evolving in a supportive way. For example, Claire's mother died from cancer when Claire was only 17 years old. Claire found a lot of support as a mother from her sisters, her mother's sisters, and her husband.

Another great place to build friendships includes houses of worship and faith communities. Many offer activities for families as well as activities for children of all ages.

There are a variety of parent organizations that you may feel connected with. These organizations can include daycare parent groups, preschool parent-teacher associations, civic organizations that cater to children, and scouting. These are just a few examples.

Community resources such as a library, recreational centers, and public parks are another way you can reach out. In addition, many community organizations run programs designed for small children and their families. This can be a great place to meet moms of other kids who are your children's age.

Professionals can also play an integral role in our Mom Community. Examples of helpful professionals include daycare providers or early learning center teachers. In addition, counselors, therapists, and psychologists often fill the Wise Woman role and can be a huge source of information specific to your child and your family's circumstances.

Life coaches can be another source of support for moms. Therapists (including psychologists) and mental health counselors assess, diagnose, and treat mental health disorders such as depression, anxiety, grief, and various life adjustment issues. On the other hand, life coaches cannot assess, diagnose, or treat mental health disorders.

Life coaches, however, assist clients in identifying specific goals for self-improvement or change and assist them in achieving those goals (Cauldwell, 2019). Life coaches can help you with specific areas of your life or problems you want to address. I like to think of psychology as a full-length mirror that allows you to see most of yourself, while coaching is like a makeup mirror that helps you zero in on one specific area.

Once you have people in your network, you have to build a community. Creating a Mom Community can feel daunting. Some moms have a built-in network of friends already (if you do, that is awesome!). If you don't, no worries, you can create one.

Here's how.

Know Your Friend's Strengths And Your Own

Without realizing it, a loving, supportive mother tends to play multiple (if not all) of the roles mentioned earlier in this book. Not because she is superhuman, but because of the longstanding close nature of the relationship. Few people (if any) in the world know us in the same way that a healthy, loving mother does. If your mother is emotionally unhealthy or the relationship has been toxic, then you already know she doesn't fit all of the mom roles mentioned in the last chapter. She may not fit even one of them.

In healthy, supportive mother/daughter relationships, one can easily rely on her mother to assist in day-to-day tasks and she fills the Go-Getter role relatively quickly. When I was about eight years old, my mother's parents moved into the house next door to us. I remember my nanny completing the typical parenting chores for my mom without even having to be asked. She assisted with the grocery shopping, taking my sister Jennifer and me to practices and friends' houses, and helping with laundry. Often, Nanny was the first person my mom asked for help.

Emotionally healthy moms can easily be the ones we turn to for emotional support. After all, they have been responding to our emotions since we were young. So many women can share their inner world with their mom in ways they can't with anyone else. Moms know our history and have been part of our emotional growth and maturity. They have seen our strengths, weaknesses, and vulnerabilities...and loved us regardless. For those moms without a mom in their life, the Emotional Supporter role is vital.

As human beings, the best educator is experience. So despite how "wise" your mom may or may not be, she has often learned from her own mothering experience. The knowledge and wisdom that comes from our mothers are invaluable. But, unfortunately, those separated by death or estrangement cannot tap into that wealth of knowledge.

As a college student, I would be up late at night studying. If I'm being honest, most of the time, I was up late stressing. However, I had the luxury of calling my mom at any time of the night. That is something I really miss. I felt terrible if I woke her up, but she was always so comforting and gracious about being there for me. For many motherless moms, this role can be the hardest to fill.

Most People Only Fit Some Of The Four Roles

But the reality is that most human beings (outside a loving mother/daughter relationship) don't typically meet all four roles; this is normal, appropriate, and healthy. We are not meant to fit all four categories in ordinary relationships. For example, I'm good at listening and am comfortable with other people's emotions. Therefore, I am an excellent Emotional Supporter. At this point in my life, I fit the role of a Wise Woman in many ways. And, of course, even Wise Women need other Wise Women.

Know Yourself

Conversely, I'm not a go-getter. I still have laundry in my washing machine from five days ago. I want to be a go-getter, but that just isn't who I am. So, even though I'd like to think of myself as the type of person who would do anything for a friend in need, I'm best with helping in the area of emotional support or information, not task management. I'm much better at lending support and guidance. Though my natural way of helping may not be what a friend needs at a specific time, that doesn't make me a bad friend. I'm a good friend because I help in the ways that I can.

Therefore, we need to know ourselves as well as our friends. When we take an honest look at ourselves and recognize our limitations, we can better accept our friends' strengths and weaknesses as well.

I encourage you to take an honest look at who you are, where your strengths lie, and which way of helping others feels most comfortable. You know you have found your ideal mode of helping when you experience joy and satisfaction while assisting someone. In addition, you will notice that your inner energy remains high — even if you are physically tired.

Conversely, your body will inform you when you attempt to help in a way that isn't in line with your inner nature. We all do this from time to time, and that is just fine. But, unfortunately, it is only sustainable for a short period. After that, we become depleted and may notice an increase in irritability, malaise, or even avoidance behavior. In the long run, it is better to acknowledge our limitations and offer to help in ways that are in line with our inner areas of strength.

Know Your Friends

Just like we need to know ourselves, we must understand the strengths and limitations of our friends. Please pay attention to how they relate to you. Each type of friend will have a typical way of interacting with you. The examples below are illustrative, but there will always be friends who fit into more than one type or relate differently than their inner helping style.

Wise Woman: The Wise Woman often is comfortable talking and sharing information. You are likely to find yourself doing various things with this friend. Sometimes, you may be talking and hearing a lot of helpful advice. Other times, she may be helping you with items and showing you the best way to try something new.

Emotional Supporter: The Emotional Supporter prefers to get together over coffee (or wine) or perhaps a meal and chat about how both of you are doing. She talks a lot about relationships and emotions. She will be the one that asks you how the kids are and how you feel about how they are doing. She is excellent at remembering your life's emotional ups and downs and will follow up with questions.

Go-Getter: The Go-Getter feels most comfortable while doing things. This is the friend you will typically be active doing fun stuff with. She knows what's going on in town and is a great planner. Her energy seems never-ending, and she is very generous in helping out. She may have three children and still find an extra arm to carry your diaper bag as you take your one child (unless you also are a Go-Getter). Although I am not a Go-Getter, I learned a long time ago that it doesn't do any good to try to keep up with these friends. I will always marvel at their energy and ability to get things done.

Late Night Talker: These friends only need a little sleep or sleep during off times. I was blessed with a best friend who was always up super late when my son Jackson was a baby. Her children were older teens, so the different schedules worked for us. It can also be helpful nowadays to have friends in other parts of the world who are naturally on different time schedules from us. With the ease of international communication with apps such as WhatsApp, Voxer, Marco Polo, and Facebook Messenger, this type of communication is becoming more accessible and more fulfilling. For example, I have two friends, one in Scotland and the other in Australia, and we use WhatsApp to help support each other as we go through various life challenges.

Support Strategy

One of the biggest hang-ups that moms have in asking for help is the idea that they don't want to burden anyone. The belief that our needs burden others, of course, is just false. The simple act of asking for help doesn't make someone else's life more difficult. Remember, they always have the ability to say yes or no.

As a mom without a mom, I felt guilty about asking people to help me. I had this notion that I should be able to care for my family independently. There was something wrong with me that I needed help. I recognize now how that belief is ridiculous. We're not burdens. After all, how often do we feel burdened when a friend asks us for help?

We demonstrate our strength when we acknowledge our limitations and seek the appropriate assistance. The following strategy is super helpful in alleviating the discomfort that will still creep up when I need extra help.

1. Identify four people you can ask to help you for one hour a month. I don't care how busy you are. None of us would bat an eyelash if a friend asked us to help them for one hour once a month, right? Once a month for an hour is nothing.

2. Schedule one friend a week for each of the four weeks that month.

When we schedule four people over the span of a month, we can have help for an hour every week. And that takes a massive load off of us.

And the act of asking for and receiving help deepens relationships. We become better at assisting others as well. We are made to live in community, and thus we are most true to who we are when we come together.

REFERENCES

Cauldwell, B. (2019). *Difference between therapy, counseling, and life coaching*. SimplePractice. Retrieved January 22, 2023 from https://www.simplepractice.com/blog/whats-the-difference-between-therapy-counseling-coaching/?utm_source=-google&utm_medium=cpc&network=x&utm_campaign=P-max_telehealth&utm_term=&device=c&matchtype=&gclid=C-jwKCAiA2rOeBhAsEiwA2Pl7QxEL8l4MC3cPhOMK5bXVN-wy--ZhTDML1mtl6JDZKCHVYILq0cTxgfRoCMqgQAvD_BwE

CHAPTER 9

CREATING A MOM IDENTITY

Growing up, my mother was larger than life. Almost literally. She was 5'10", and I was a pretty small girl for my age. But she also had a larger-than-life personality. She had a commanding presence and was known by almost everyone in our small rural town in the Catskill Mountains of New York. She wore many hats and had several careers in her short 51 years. She was a real estate broker and owned her own real estate business. She was the captain of the local ambulance squad and became first an emergency medical technician (EMT) and then an EMT instructor. She obtained a commercial driver's license, became a school bus driver, and then became a driving instructor. Finally, she ran for and was elected our town magistrate. My mother didn't just do things; she led things.

I was known simply as one of Sue Derby's girls. Being my mother's daughter was one of the primary aspects of my identity for the first 25 years of my life. My mom was my caregiver, my role model, and my hero. I wanted to be just like her and believed that she could do no wrong.

And then, I became a young adult myself and learned that she, like most of us, had her own scars and wounds. She lived with her own early life traumas and mental health issues. I discovered that this woman whom I idolized was as broken as I felt (and in many ways more so).

And then I became a mom. How would I learn to be a mom without my mom to show me? Did I want to be a mom just like her? Was I going to do things differently?

Now that I was a mom, I became painfully aware of some of the struggles she had. I wondered what it was like for her to be pregnant as a young woman. Was she scared? Who supported her? What was it like? I wanted to know how she healed from her miscarriage. How did she handle the sleepless nights? Why did she decide to bottle feed rather than breast feed? I didn't even know her birth stories.

I never knew my mom as a woman or what it was like for her to be a mother. Sadly, I wasn't even aware of how little I knew about her in this way. All I knew was what it was like to be her daughter.

My mom had a difficult life, including physical abuse, neglect, significant poverty, and growing up in an alcoholic home, followed by the death of her oldest child and her own medical concerns. I spent years watching her relationship with her mother (my nanny). Their relationship had its ups and downs. They were very different women, and I know my mother worked hard to be different from her own mother when raising her girls. I never truly understood the nature of her grief and its impact on her life, including her mood, emotions, sense of herself as a mom, physical health, and mental health.

THRIVING AS A MOM WITHOUT A MOM

What Is Identity And How Is It Formed?

The American Psychological Association defines identity as:

> "an individual's sense of self is defined by (a) a set of physical, psychological, and interpersonal characteristics that is not wholly shared with any other person and (b) a range of affiliations (e.g., ethnicity) and social roles. Identity involves a sense of continuity or the feeling that one is the same person today that one was yesterday or last year (despite physical or other changes). Such a sense is derived from one's body sensations; body image; and the feeling that one's memories, goals, values, expectations, and beliefs belong to the self" American Psychological Association. (n.d.).

We aren't born knowing who we are. Our early life experiences, the environments we grow up in, and the people we are raised with all influence our sense of self. We learn about ourselves by learning how we are similar and different from other people in our lives.

Ego identity is defined by Erikson (1980) as "The accrued confidence that one's ability to maintain inner sameness and continuity is matched by the sameness and continuity of one's meaning for others" (94-95). In other words, your identity is related to how similar or dissimilar you view yourself as compared to other groups of people (Derby, 1998). Therefore, your identity as a mom is connected with our perception of what it means to be a mom and our observations of other moms.

As a mom, I know you have witnessed your children mimic your behavior. I remember how cute I thought it was when my two-year-old son Jackson would pretend to vacuum with me each time

I pulled out the vacuum. This isn't something I taught him to do; he just did it. A child's brain is wired to mimic and copy the actions and behaviors of adults. Every human does this automatically.

Even in adulthood, we continue to use other people as models for our behavior. Ironically, we don't even recognize the fact that we're doing it (and let's face it, every teenager out there thinks they are entirely original). Becoming a mom isn't any different from other new behaviors. Our brain automatically wants to learn from what it has observed others doing.

Personality Traits, Values, And Behaviors

Personality traits are the stable inclinations, temperament, and dispositions that represent who we are (Czerniawska & Szydło, 2021). Therefore, when we think about who we are, it is our personality that we often think about.

Values are stable and also represent what we favor. (Czerniawska & Szydło, 2021). The Merriam-Webster Dictionary defines values as "something (such as a principle or quality) intrinsically valuable or desirable" (Merriam-Webster, n.d.). Values are beliefs that are firm, not rigid convictions. Values can be positive, which are constructive and health-promoting, or harmful, which are destructive and unhealthy. Values are something you care about — a lot. Values measure what people feel are desirable, vital, functional, and worthwhile. They influence how we feel, think, make choices, perform, and behave (Ninivaggi, 2016).

Personality traits, values, and behaviors interact to form the basis for how we show up in the world. I will use myself as an example of how the three aspects of the self interact. I am an introvert, which is a personality trait, while compassion is one of my core values. My introverted personality trait means that I am energized by alone time and value deep, meaningful connections with others. I like to ponder and think about things, and feel things deeply. Although I am fine being in large groups of people, I am drained quickly and need to replenish myself by spending time alone. I live out my value of compassion by connecting with those in need, asking about their welfare, and providing assistance. Behaviors used in living out this value include being polite and choosing my words carefully while still being direct.

You can share personality traits and values with your mother, and choose to behave in very different ways from her.

For example, my mom was a yeller and easily angered. I was determined not to be like that with my own children. Most of you would agree that minimizing those behaviors is a great goal, and they are. However, I didn't recognize how much I was dampening all of my intense emotions. My personality flattened after I became a mom.

After a lot of personal work, I realized that part of who my mom was, and who I am, is a passionate and deeply emotional person, and that feeling and expressing emotions deeply was part of who we are. Through my own therapy and coaching, I have been able to regulate my emotions so that I can still feel and express emotions deeply while staying calm and peaceful when it comes to parenting. Sadly, my mother didn't have the opportunity to do the personal work needed, and the intensity of her emotions spilled out on us as children through hurtful behaviors.

I can now embrace my passionate nature and express my emotions in a way that doesn't hurt my children. I have learned to identify when my system is overloaded with feelings and to calm my body (specifically my nervous system) before I engage with my family. It isn't the emotion or passion that I need to be different; it is the behaviors that I need to be different. In other words, It is the behavior (yelling) that should be different, not the personality trait (emotionally passionate).

Mom Identity Issues For Moms Whose Moms Are Physically Separated From Them

For many moms, physical distance from their mothers doesn't impact how they view themselves as a mom. However, distance can create unexpected and unique challenges with identity. For example, complications with identity can occur if the women live in different cultures or experience vastly different lifestyles.

For example, Janice, a 28-year-old mom of a toddler I interviewed, was living in an impoverished rural community in South America as part of a two-year mission program while her mother was living in an urban setting in the Northeast of the United States. Janice struggled with her sense of who she was as a mom because her childhood experience and her mother's advice and guidance were so different from what she was experiencing in her home and foreign community. As a result, she was embracing a more communal stance in her parenting — which wasn't consistent with her family of origin.

Another potentially tricky situation occurs if your parents come in and out of your life. Again, this can disrupt the flow of the family dynamics and influence how a mom feels about herself.

Mom Identity Issues For Moms Who Are Estranged Or Choose To Have Limited Contact Due To An Unhealthy Relationship

There were many years in which I wanted to be very different from my mom. I saw her as a self-focused martyr who couldn't see how her dysfunction impacted me. During my most distressed moments, I was angry at her for being a wounded, flawed mess.

In my 20s, I had very little compassion for the struggles she was experiencing. I was sure that I wasn't going to do to my kids what she did to me. I wasn't going to give them the silent treatment or a significant guilt trip anytime they didn't make me happy. I wasn't going to live vicariously through my children's achievements and place the heavy burden of success on them. I wasn't going to leave them alone at a young age and make them responsible for cooking and cleaning.

And then I became a mom. I now had a new understanding of how a mom could be insecure. For some reason, I thought that once you were a mom, confidence just came...almost like magic. It's been over 20 years since my mother died. I have had a long time to work through my anger and frustration over what I saw as poor parenting.

For the purposes of this book, I define an unhealthy relationship as one in which you experience repeated and/or prolonged periods of devaluation, emotional manipulation, emotional abuse, or other circumstances that lead to emotional harm or risk to your mental health. Several circumstances contribute to a person being emotionally abusive or neglectful. Examples include a history of abuse or neglect, early childhood trauma, and mental illness. It is important to note that the experience of these things does not mean that one will become emotionally abusive; it simply means they are vulnerable to it. This is similar to someone with a parent with heart disease; it doesn't mean that they will have heart disease, it just means that they are more vulnerable to it.

I know that many of you continue to have problematic and even toxic relationships with your mothers. The anger and continued emotional warfare in emotionally abusive or estranged relationships between mothers and daughters can make it difficult for you to embrace aspects of yourself as a mom. You have been the recipient of emotional pain at your mother's hand, and you want to ensure you don't continue this pattern in your own family.

For example, Mia's mother initially abandoned her in infancy and then repeatedly re-entered Mia's life and brought chaos, neglect, and abuse. Mia found that the name Mom or Mother was triggering for her.

"I didn't realize how much my relationship with my mom impacted me until I had my daughter in 2018," Mia said. "I had postpartum and was struggling with whether to stay or go. After that, I knew what 'go' felt like. I hated being a mother. For me, a mother is someone who hurts, leaves, and abandons."

It is essential to stop cycles of abuse, and the moms I've worked with and interviewed for this book have put considerable effort into being different from their mothers. Unfortunately, when you focus on being different from someone, you run the risk of becoming inauthentic or cutting yourself off from a vital aspect of your personality like I did with passionate emotions.

Remember, you can have similar values or personality traits and consciously choose to behave differently. I learned to embrace passion as a personality trait my mother and I shared, but I did not allow that trait to manifest itself in yelling or cruel discipline—regardless of the intensity of my own emotional responses to things.

It is normal to have different values from our parents or even to prioritize our values differently. However, when values dramatically clash, it can be difficult to feel close to that person or understand and respect their perspective. Unfortunately, this is often at the heart of most estrangements.

You never need to justify your value system to others, including extended family members. It isn't your responsibility to get them to see, understand, or agree with what you see as important.

However, you are responsible for living out your values.

You never need to stay connected with people who jeopardize your physical or mental health. Your children will thrive best when you are physically, emotionally, mentally, and spiritually healthy. Your well-being is essential; therefore, if you need to separate yourself from your mother to be healthy, that is not only okay — it is appropriate and beneficial for your children.

Mom Identity Issues For Moms Whose Mothers Have Died

Developing an identity as a mom is complicated when your mother has died, regardless of your prior relationship. Feelings of grief can alter your recollections and intensify unresolved issues, even when the relationship is healthy. In addition, guilt and remorse can easily pop up since there isn't the ability to say the things left unsaid or do the things you had hoped to do before her death.

Many times I have laughed over the notion of becoming my mother. All of us, at one time or another, have seen the cliche references of women teasing themselves about how one day they woke up and realized they had become their mothers.

These cliches exist because it is typical to emulate some aspects of our mother as we become a mother ourselves. We all do it, whether we recognize it or not. It is hard-wired into our neurology. But this doesn't mean that we are a carbon copy of our mother, nor does it mean that we aren't able to intentionally be different from her.

History Of A Healthy Maternal Relationship

One of the potential complicating factors for a mom who has had a healthy relationship with her mother involves negatively comparing herself to an idolized memory. You may feel like you need to live up to your mother's standards, for example. As a result, you may criticize each decision or parenting judgment that you make. Or perhaps you need more time to make the right choice over the fear of making the wrong choice. These feelings and experiences can lead to sadness, insecurity, and low self-esteem.

Another concern for moms in this situation is the potential to become constrained by what you remember your mom as being. You may limit aspects of yourself in order to not deviate from your mom's way of being, which leads to ignoring parts of yourself or changing the way you want to parent. Since you are denying part of yourself, you don't feel authentic or genuine. You may recognize feelings of being an imposter or feel like you are always putting on an act.

It can feel like walking a fine line between being yourself versus being who you think you should be based on how your mom was. Hailey described her experience with this, "There are a lot of times I feel like I'm not doing the best job. But then there are a lot of times I look at what she did and realize that I don't want my life to be only about being a mom."

Another potential issue relates to feelings of betrayal. I've interviewed several women who felt like they were betraying their mother by doing things differently from how she did them. When your mom isn't living, it is harder to get the reassurance that parenting in a way consistent with your values isn't a sign of betrayal. Instead, it represents a healthy way of parenting that should be supported.

History Of Unhealthy Maternal Relationships

If you are one of the many women who have experienced an unhealthy relationship with your mother, there are several things to consider regarding developing your mom identity. First, as mentioned above, I define an unhealthy relationship as one in which you experience repeated and/or prolonged devaluation, emotional manipulation, emotional abuse, or other circumstances that lead to emotional harm or risk to your mental health.

No one should endure this type of treatment, especially at their mother's hand. When it occurs, it often leaves emotional wounds that require healing. The process of healing from emotional abuse at the hands of one's mother is not within the scope of this book. Psychotherapy or coaching can be really valuable in healing wounds caused by early life experiences.

Some women report greater freedom in being themselves now that their mother is deceased.

For Claire, she found that anger and pain were part of her sense of self as she became a mom.

She stated, "I'm angry I don't have a mother to call on. It's become my character, my identity. Sometimes it feels like, 'Will this pain ever end?' The pain was all new again all the time when my kids were young."

Isabelle reported that her mother was emotionally unhealthy and died when she was 11. She questioned who she, Isabelle, was and felt like she was.

She said, "Just trying to find out who I was. I tried to figure out my identity. I never counted on other people; I just did it myself."

Later, after becoming a mom herself, Isabelle struggled with what it meant to be a good mom: "Was I a good mom? Because I don't know; I didn't have one."

Fortunately, some women report greater freedom in being themselves after their mother is deceased.

Chloe stated this so eloquently when she said, "I try and draw from the things my mom did right, and I try to have that life in me. And the things she did wrong I use as fuel for me to be more self-aware and more intentional of my experience of motherhood and my daughter's experience of childhood. I take more responsibility for my role. We don't have to be perfect, but we must be accountable for our actions."

REFERENCES

American Psychological Association. (n.d.) *APA Dictionary of Psychology*. American Psychological Association. Retrieved January 22, 2023 from https://dictionary.apa.org/identity

Czerniawska, M. & Szydło, J. (2021). Do Values Relate to Personality Traits and if so, in What Way? — Analysis of Relationships. *Psychology research and behavior management, 14*, 511-527. Retrieved January 22, 2023 from https://doi.org/10.2147/PRBM.S299720

Derby, M. (1999). *The effects of a ruminative response style of depression on adolescent self-concept development.* University of Hartford ProQuest Dissertations Publishing.

Erikson, E. (1980). *Identity and the life cycle.* Norton.

Merriam-Webster. (n.d.) *Values definition & meaning.* Retrieved January 22, 2023 from https://www.merriam-webster.com/dictionary/values#dictionary-entry-1

Ninivaggi, F. (2016). Values 101. *Psychology Today*. Retrieved January 22, 2023 from https://www.psychologytoday.com/us/blog/envy/201612/values-101

CHAPTER 10

HOW TO CREATE A MOM IDENTITY YOU LOVE

I dentity is something we create. We are the author of our own book. There is no right way to be a mom. Each of us is unique, and we must have a sense of ourselves that makes us feel proud. To feel good about who we are as a mom, we need to identify our values.

Values Journal

To embrace your values, you first need to know what they are. Creating a values journal can be a helpful way to figure this out. Follow these easy steps to create your own values journal. You will find a list of values at the end of this chapter, which can help you get started if you need it.

1. Designate a large section of an existing journal or get yourself a new journal specifically for your values. I am partial to making journals special (I like pretty covers with fancy paper) because your writing is special.

2. Identify the values you hold dear and put one on each page. Don't overthink this step; put down any value that pops into your mind. You can add additional values over time, so you don't have to worry if you miss something. Remember, these are values you see in yourself, don't think about whether other people would agree with you.

3. Each night, reflect on your day and jot down examples of how you lived out at least one of your values. For example, today I held the door open for an older adult as she left the grocery store. I then helped her load her bags into her car. This is an example of my value of kindness. This step is essential, so don't skip it. You will feel secure and confident in your values when you see concrete evidence of how you live them out.

4. Periodically reflect (I like doing this monthly) on your journal, so you can see which values you most strongly connect with. You may or may not be surprised by what you see. Remember, there are no right or wrong values, but how we live or don't live them out can impact how we feel. For example, I may value kindness — but I may live out that value with strangers more than with my family. When I notice this pattern, I can put more effort into being kind to the people I love.

5. Make minor adjustments in your behavior to align with the values that you want to prioritize.

As I mentioned earlier, values are neither bad nor good. It is your behavior that is healthy or unhealthy, bad or good, functional or dysfunctional. For example, the value of independence is good and reasonable. However, how you live it out can look very different from how someone else lives it. Furthermore, the parenting choices we make can be very different based on the age of our child, even if we maintain the same values.

For example, my son Jackson is 11 years old and is completely capable of making himself peanut butter toast. He has done it many times when he is by himself without complaint. However, there are times when I am busy and he asks for peanut butter toast. I will let him know that he has to make it himself. Whether he chooses to make it is up to him. Regardless of how much he whines and complains, if I am busy, I don't make it for him. That same scenario would be inappropriate if my son was four and didn't have the skills to make his snack independently.

Incorporating Values In Parenting

All moms get bombarded with parenting advice even before the baby is born. It is hard to know whose advice to trust, and the amount of information available on Google is overwhelming. Since we don't have a mom to bounce ideas off of, we are left to ourselves to figure out what advice to follow.

Even the soundest advice and healthiest parenting styles aren't appropriate for every mother. Being a mom is not a one-size fits-all experience. We all want to be fulfilled, competent, and loving moms. Unfortunately, there needs to be a manual teaching us how (despite the thousands of techniques and informational videos we see on social media).

It can be easy to feel like a feather in the wind getting blown around each time we see an intriguing technique on TikTok or read about the latest trend in parenting. Add on the burden of not having your mom to bounce things off. What's a mom to do?

The answer is to make decisions based on your values and priorities. When you are faced with a decision or a challenge, consider your values. As you write in your values journal and reflect over time, you will notice several values that tend to be primary in your life. When you base your decisions on your values, you can be confident that you are doing the right thing for yourself and your family — even if it looks different from the advice you are receiving or how your mother did things.

There will be times when you have equally important values that appear to be conflicting. When this occurs, you need to decide which is of higher priority in each particular instance. For example, two of my values are compassion and fairness. And at times I have made decisions that weren't fair to some because it was the more compassionate choice.

For example, my family always gets a disability pass for my son Jackson when we go to an amusement park. Having the pass makes the entire experience easier for him and reduces some of the challenges he experiences based on his neurological differences. This isn't fair to the other people in line, especially the other children who also hate waiting. I choose to get the pass every time because I see my son working harder to do things other kids do routinely without even thinking about it. So, if my son can have an easier time of things at an amusement park, I make it happen. Here I choose compassion for the effort my son exhibits in everyday life over fairness.

There will also be times when your values conflict with someone else's values. This can be tricky if you are co-parenting with the other person. If not, remember, you are the parent and ultimately it is your values that are the most important. Don't question your-self simply because someone you respect has different opinions.

However, it can get tricky if you are co-parenting with someone and the two of you disagree.

For example, closeness and connection are two high-prior-ity values in my life. Safety, independence, and self-reliance are high-priority values for my husband. All of these are beautiful values and essential in parenting.

Unfortunately, they clashed a bit regarding our different opin-ions on our infant's nighttime behavior. It was important to me to co-sleep with Jackson, but my husband Tom was uncomfort-able with that decision. Both of us had very sound reasons for choosing our preferred sleeping environment. We decided that Jackson and I would sleep separately from Tom, so that all of us were comfortable. Jackson had developed a healthy sleep routine and could transition to his crib at 10 months, and I returned to sleeping with Tom.

Both my husband and I hold the five values mentioned above (closeness, connection, safety, independence, and self-reliance) as essential and as part of our personal value system. However, we prioritize them a bit differently — so the parenting choices we make sometimes look different. Yet, when you stay true to your values, your choices will align with who you are and your comfort and confidence in parenting will grow.

As a parent, you will be faced with challenging choices.

- How do I feed my baby?
- What sleep environment do I create?
- Which parenting style works best for me?
- Do I let my child sleep at a friend's house?

- Do I choose a babysitter who isn't part of my family?

- Do I let my child vacation with other family members?

- How important are grades in our family?

No matter how old our children are, we will always face new challenges and questions that we need to answer for ourselves. The good news is that we don't need to know the answers. When unsure, ask yourself which response or solution best aligns with what is important to you. And then feel comfortable knowing that you are making the best choice you can.

Values

Accountability	Adventure	Authenticity	Awareness
Balanced life	Beauty	Boldness	Bravery
Calmness	Challenge	Cleanliness	Confidence
Compassion	Community	Commitment	Connection
Contentment	Cooperation	Courage	Creativity
Curiosity	Decisiveness	Democracy	Dependability
Determination	Dignity	Diligence	Discipline
Discovery	Diversity	Duty	Education
Empathy	Encouragement	Equality	Excellence
Experience	Expertise	Exploration	Fairness
Faith	Family	Flexibility	Focus
Forgiveness	Freedom	Friendship	Frugality
Fulfillment	Fun	Generosity	Gratitude
Grooming	Growth	Happiness	Health
Helpfulness	Honesty	Hopefulness	Humility

Humor	Integrity	Intentionality	Intimacy
Intuition	Justice	Kindness	Knowledge
Leadership	Learning	Love	Loyalty
Mindfulness	Moderation	Motivation	Openness
Optimism	Originality	Passion	Patience
Peacefulness	Persuasiveness	Professionalism	Reason
Recognition	Resilience	Respect	Responsibility
Sacrifice	Security	Self-care	Self-discipline
Self-reliance	Self-respect	Sensitivity	Sensuality
Serenity	Service	Sharing	Significance
Simplicity	Sincerity	Spirituality	Stability
Strength	Structure	Success	Support
Sympathy	Thoughtfulness	Thrift	Timeliness
Tradition	Trust	Understanding	Uniqueness
Usefulness	Virtue	Vision	Warmth
Wisdom			

CHAPTER 11

HOW TO THRIVE AS A MOM WITHOUT A MOM

Thriving as a Mom Without A Mom Framework

Hardship Is The First Step On The Path To Resilience

Resilience isn't created from an easy life. You need to overcome something difficult to grow and develop the resources to thrive despite life's challenges. As a mom who doesn't have your mom, you have already gone through hardship. How you view that experience and the meaning you give it plays a massive role in how you will feel about your life.

Viktor Frankl, a Nazi concentration camp survivor, wrote, "In some ways, suffering ceases to be suffering at the moment it finds a meaning, such as the meaning of a sacrifice" (p. 117). We don't find meaning, we create it. We choose what we think of our life and our circumstances. We have the freedom to view our life in ways that propel us forward regardless of what we've experienced in the past.

Even though being a mom without a mom has many challenges, we have an opportunity to recognize the strength and resilience that we've developed in order to survive the difficulties. The meaning we attribute to the experiences in our life plays a significant role in how we feel about ourselves and our circumstances. Below you will find several concepts that have been helpful to me and other moms as we've created ways to thrive.

Forgiveness

Some moms have found forgiveness as a means to gain control over their experiences and move forward healthily.

Mia shared with me how hard she has worked to forgive her mother despite the fact that she chooses to have no contact with her. This forgiveness has freed Mia up to be more present with her children.

She stated, "My mom wasn't good at showing up for me, so I've been very conscious about how I show up for my kids and I make sure that I am present for them as much as possible. I make a huge deal out of birthdays. I make a point to make sure my children know that the day they were born is a day to be celebrated and not ignored."

Inner Strength

Many moms I've talked to and worked with have found that as they've healed, they have been able to recognize their inner strength.

For example, Darla said, "I feel like I'm a much stronger personality. I'm confident in my decisions. I've got this."

Like Darla, Hailey sees her experience of being a mom without a mom as part of her life journey.

Hailey stated, "I wouldn't be as successful as I am; I wouldn't be helping so many people if I hadn't lost my mom. So I try and honor her in this way."

Empathy And Compassion

High levels of empathy and compassion have been a recurring theme among moms without a mom.

Angeline's mother died a couple years before she became pregnant.

Angeline said, "I think it's made me a lot more empathetic and grateful for what I do have. It makes me work harder to maintain the relationships I have. It's made me more compassionate for those people in my family. I'm more patient."

Freedom From Interference

Some women feel good about the freedom from interference they experience.

For example, Claire stated, "I am nothing at all like my mom. If my mother had lived, I don't think we would have gotten along at all. I think she would have interfered a lot. I would tell myself things like 'I don't have that burden or obligation of my mom' to try and feel better."

Angeline, who was in the advanced stages of pregnancy when we spoke, also believes that she will have an easier time being the mother she wants to be without feeling guilty that she is parenting differently than her mother did.

She said, "I feel some kind of relief, like I can just do it my way without having to explain myself. I want to be a gentler parent and a more empathic parent."

Goal Setting

Goal setting can be another valuable tool for building resiliency. Goals are both long-term and short-term, and setting both types can be helpful.

Olivia reported that as an entrepreneur, goal setting has been a tool that she is very comfortable with.

She stated thar her main goal is for "my kids to be healthy adults and give them all the tools to cope with the reality of being an adult. Having that clear goal in mind has helped me be the best mom I can be."

Olivia's example illustrates a long-term goal. Short-term goals include nursing for the first six months, re-evaluating a decision you've made, or getting your child to 90% of this season's sports or dance practices.

Self-Growth

The hardship of being a mom without a mom can be a catalyst for self-growth.

Chloe said, "The biggest lessons were that personal responsibility means taking responsibility for my physical health as well as my mental health, emotions, and reactions. It pushes me to be the healthiest I can be. That is why I have been so focused on somatic work."

Once you've done the work, even though you may never have the mom you wish you could have, you can still feel great about who you are as a mom and thrive.

Teaching Opportunity

Creating meaning from your experiences can be healing for you and your children.

For example, Leslie found comfort in talking about her late mother to her daughter and has found conversations about death to be a way to decrease the stigma of death.

Leslie stated, "I now talk to the older one about death and dying. It is opening up a dialogue about that. What is death, why do people die, and what about God? We visit my mom in the cemetery. I think it will help her as we have had these conversations."

Advice From Moms Without A Mom

I have offered strategies, tips, and advice throughout this book. In addition, I have had the privilege of getting advice from several other moms without a mom and I want to share that advice with you. Each woman was asked to give any advice she thought would be helpful to you, and here is what they said in their own words.

"I would just say hang in there. It's hard. It's very, very hard. Make friends if you can. Be involved with as many things as you can with your kids. Find your people and hold them close. Know that you can do it by yourself. It's hard, but you've got it. It will come eventually; keep going. Go to counseling if you can." ~ Darla

"Find another mom without a mom. Most people don't understand. My advice, what helped me the most, was finding a surrogate important female whom I trusted — preferably a woman maybe 5 to 10 years older. I had two such friends plus my mother's surviving older sister. My aunt was priceless and my friends were like big sisters to me. They made all the difference in the world. I don't think I could have survived without them." ~ Claire

"Don't despair; I know it's hard to find the support network where you are. Don't feel like it's a replacement, because nothing is a replacement. Just build helpful relationships. Don't feel like you have to idealize that relationship." ~ Carmen

"Find community. Love yourself and care for yourself first." ~ Mia

"Let them know they are not alone." ~ Isabelle

"I'm a big believer in counseling and coaching. Surround yourself with other people who understand you. You need to grieve and understand those feelings. You have to learn to move forward." ~ Hailey

"If there is a way to celebrate her life with your kids in order to keep that memory alive, maybe that would be helpful for everyone. I find I over-document everything. I don't want my girls to have the experience I've had; I want them to have the information I didn't." ~ Leslie

"You can lose anything in life. You need to hold onto your faith. God is the only thing you can't lose. It's the one thing no one can take away from me." ~ Angeline

"Don't beat yourself up about it. Have compassion for yourself. Journal, write letters to your mom. It helps me process things, and it's like I'm talking to her. Talking to your child about Grandma, so your kids can identify with that role. Find community with other motherless moms." ~ Beth

"It's important to build a village of supportive people who have your kid's best interests at heart. Keep seeking healing, whether it is physical or mental. Don't be afraid to break the cycles. Don't be afraid to say no and set boundaries. Or to say yes, to let yourself try things; don't let your traumas hold you back from doing things that you can." ~ Olivia

"Don't forget to put yourself first. We can't fill up other people if we don't fill ourselves up. That means dealing with the feelings and emotions as they come, instead of pushing them down." ~ Sophia

"To try and find a support system whereever they can. Not just online, but have women they can turn to in their life that they can be supported by. Turn grief and loss into a tool. Use it as a mechanism to be the best mom they can be for their children. There are lessons tucked away in pain. It can make them a better mom; they just need to uncover what those lessons are." ~ Chloe

"Just remember love comes first! Including loving yourself. Love first, everything else second. Lean on God and talk to Jesus everyday. Prayer is powerful. Stop and breathe. Breathe deep. Breathe often. Just breathe. It's good for your body and soul. Same with dance. Dance often with your kiddos. Laugh with your kiddos every chance you get. Laughter really is good medicine. Laughter is also good for your soul and family. Get outdoors. Go on adventures. See the great things about your town, your county, and your state. Road trips are the best. Do lots of them. Adventures make the best memories as well as activities like crafts and games and puzzles and playtime. Family dinners and creative conversations. Do what's right for you and your family! Care for one another. Much love and happiness." ~ Rivke

Additional Tools Specifically For Moms Without A Mom

Although no one can ever take the place of a loving mom, I want you to know that you aren't alone. You are part of the Moms Without A Mom Club, and we are here for you. My hope is that you've found both knowledge and support from this book.

In addition to this book, I have created the following resources designed specifically for moms without a mom that you can access.

The Mom Without A Mom Quiz

Uncover how being a mom without a mom is affecting you. Being a mom when you don't have a mom to turn to can be difficult. Access the free quiz at this URL: https://bit.ly/momswithoutamomquiz to learn more about how it's affecting your motherhood journey and what you can do to reclaim your joy.

Enjoy Being A Mom Again Free Quick Guide

Have you had the experience of playing with your child or just watching them sleep, and suddenly a memory involving your mom will pop into your mind? Or perhaps while you are with your child, you notice being distracted by thoughts in your head — including conversations you've had or would like to have with your mom?

It is typical for thoughts and memories to be triggered spontaneously. Sometimes, these thoughts and memories are pleasant and we welcome them. Other times they can create sadness, pain, or even anger. All moms separated from their mothers by death, estrangement, or physical distance experience this.

This guide gives you the five-step process to go from being distracted to present with your children. You can access the guide at this URL: https://bit.ly/Enjoy-motherhood-guide.

Care For Yourself While You Care For Your Baby Free Guide

As moms, we know how valuable our time is and often we find ourselves with very little of it. We have all heard how important self-care is and I would guess that you already know that (or you wouldn't be reading this now). You don't have to carve out time away from your child to take care of yourself (because let's face it, sometimes time alone is not an option!). You can engage in self-care without leaving your baby. Yes, you can!

This guide contains easy strategies to take care of yourself while you not only care for your baby, but also create strong lasting and healthy emotional bonds. You can access the guide at this URL: https://bit.ly/Self-care-with-Baby-Guide

Mom Community Checklist

None of us want to think about what happens when something goes wrong, but when our children's safety is at stake it is vital that we plan ahead. Are you ready for when an emergency arises?

- Do you lack the support and guidance of a caring mother in your day-to-day life?

- Do you dread having an emergency because you don't know who you will call for help?

- Do you avoid creating a support network because you don't even know where to start?

This checklist makes it simple to prepare for when you need help unexpectedly. You can access the checklist at this URL: https://bit.ly/Mom-checklist

Private Free Facebook Community

We all know being a mom is hard. But being a mom without the support and guidance of a loving mom by your side is even harder. Every mom without a mom needs a community where she can feel supported, seek advice, and benefit from the wisdom of other moms who have been there. This small and active group is the perfect place for all moms without a mom to hang out. Access the group at this URL: http://bit.ly/3RdZk9F

Complimentary Coaching Call

I want all moms to thrive and recognize their inner strength, especially those moms like me who don't have a loving, supportive mom in their day-to-day lives.

We are all stronger when we have a community that understands us!

Here is your personal invitation to schedule a time for us to talk. Use this URL: https://bit.ly/Call-Melissa-Reilly

Moms Without A Mom Website

I encourage you to take a look at my website: www.
momswithoutamom.com. There you will find my coaching
programs designed specifically for moms without a mom, my
monthly blog, and workshops and courses all focused on moms
without a mom.

Conclusion

We all know that being a mom is hard. But being a mom without
the support and guidance of a loving mom in your day-to-day life
is even harder.

Moms without a mom don't have the go-to person most mothers function as. We can't easily tap into our mom's wisdom when
we need it. We don't have a loving mother by our side to use as
a mirror while trying to figure out who we are as moms. And we
have the added drain from grieving the absence of what we want,
a loving mom by our side as we navigate the world of motherhood.

The great news is that by following these three steps: 1) recognizing and healing those unexpected moments of grief; 2) intentionally building your Mom Community; and 3) actively reflecting
upon and creating your mom identity, you will thrive as a mom
without a mom. Furthermore, you will experience motherhood's
usual ups and downs and feel good about who you are as a mom.

REFERENCES

Frankl, V. (1984). *Man's search for meaning: an introduction to logo-therapy.* 3rd ed. Simon & Schuster.

ACKNOWLEDGMENTS

First and foremost, I want to thank all of the moms without a mom who strive to be the best mom you can be. I especially want to thank those women who so generously gave their time to share their stories with me for this book. You are an amazing bunch of women who inspire me.

Thank you to my wonderful writing coach and editor Stephanie Mojica. Your guidance, support, and expertise allowed me to make the lifelong wish to write a book a reality.

Thank you, Asya Blue, for the book design and for taking my words and putting them into a book that looks great.

I am very appreciative to the following women who read and offered feedback: Adrianne Hart, Dana Malstaff, Fiona Valentine, Nicole Terrell, Emilie Delworth, Denise Takakjy, and Sandra Pezzillo. Your kindness and support mean the world to me!

I owe a debt of gratitude to Tara Reid, Nicole Liloia, and Dana Malstaff, my business coaches who not only helped me see the direction I wanted to go, but also taught me the ins and outs of the online business world. Thank you for sharing your knowledge and guidance.

I have been blessed with an amazing group of businesswomen who have walked with me on my journey into online coaching: Adrianne Hart, Fiona Valentine, and Laura Cunningham. Your support, encouragement, and feedback along the way has been invaluable.

I am blessed with a wonderful faith community through which I gain strength and comfort every day. Thank you to the leadership and congregation of St. Paul Evangelical Lutheran Church in Lititz, PA for lifting me up when I've needed it. And I acknowledge and celebrate God's spirit working within me always.

As a mom without a mom, I have had to rely on my friends for assistance as well as emotional support. Whenever I needed anything, I knew one of you would be available to help me. God has blessed me with the best friends I could ever hope to have. I will forever be in your debt, Kimberly Todd, Emily Myallis, Elaine Bell, and Brenda Penny.

BethAnn Shoudt, Psy.D., I can't imagine having a better business partner. Your belief in me and your support has been a buoy in rough waters. I have always valued your wisdom and encouragement. Thank you!

Lorin and Craig Levins, you have been with me through most of my journey. The geographic distance has never mattered in our friendship and knowing that I always have the two of you in my corner has provided me with the strength and courage to reach for the stars. Thank you both for always being there!

I want to thank my father John Derby and Janet Derby for your continued support and encouragement through the years. It has meant the world to me. I love you!

To my amazing Aunt Sandra, you have been my biggest supporter, best friend, confidant, role model, and the dearest aunt I could ever have. You and Jim have been there for me when I've needed it the most, and I can never thank the two of you enough. I am eternally grateful! I love you!

Jackson and Tommy, the two of you are great boys and I am so proud to call you my sons! I love you!

And finally, to my husband, Tom. I am so glad that we are walking this journey together. Thank you for believing in me. I love you!

ABOUT THE AUTHOR

Melissa E. D. Reilly, Psy.D., is the mom of two boys, a clinical psychologist, and a coach for moms without a mom. As a mom without a mom herself, she is passionate about helping other moms who don't have the support and guidance of a loving mother by their side thrive. In her spare time, she enjoys reading, spending time in nature, being active in her Lutheran church, and having fun with her husband, two boys, and two dogs.

Melissa's psychological practice, Shoudt & Reilly Psychological Services, has been serving residents of Berks County, Pennsylvania, for over 23 years. She is now expanding her services to include coaching for moms without a mom, which can be accessed by women worldwide through her website momswithoutamom.com.